HERITAGE
CROCHET:
AN ANALYSIS

Mary Konior

Dryad Press Ltd   London

ACKNOWLEDGMENT

With sincere thanks to: Patricia Knowlden, first of all, for allowing me to use her collection of crochet; Wilhelmena Curtis, Joan Edwards, Winifred Paine and Joan Walker for their gifts; Jenifer Frost for information on Flora Klickmann; Muriel Gahan, of the Royal Dublin Society for her searches among the society's archives; Joan Kendall for information on the conservation of lace; Carl Konior for his assistance in locating obscure data; J. & P. Coats (UK) Ltd for information on their products; the Fabric Care Research Association Ltd for advice; Patons & Baldwins Ltd for information on their publications; and to all others whose brains I have picked or whose gifts I have not otherwise acknowledged. Occasionally when lecturing I have found myself the recipient of a specimen of old crochet, and as I did not consciously set out to collect crochet, to my shame, I did not always record the name of the donor. The collection just grew, and often a new addition has been accompanied by the request, 'Please give it a good home'. I have.

Illustrations 6, 14 and 22 are reproduced by courtesy of the Board of Trustees of the Victoria and Albert Museum.

ISBN 0 8521 9642 3

Typeset by Tek-Art Ltd, Kent
and printed in Great Britain by
Anchor Brendon Ltd
Tiptree, Essex
for the publishers
Dryad Press Ltd.
8 Cavendish Square
London W1M 0AJ

CONTENTS

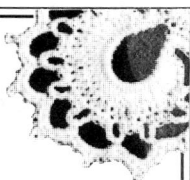

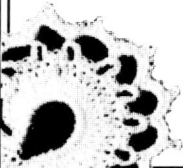

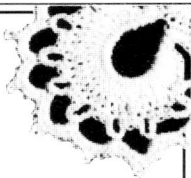

INTRODUCTION

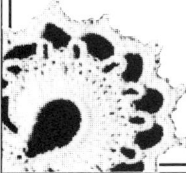

There is a rich heritage of old crochet. The extent and depth of its richness is not always appreciated, for the subject is perhaps one of life's lesser antiquities. This book is an attempt to display some of the treasure, so that readers can identify various styles of crochet and perhaps re-create some of the laces for themselves.

The field is vast in the quest for old crochet; it rises to the fore in Victoriana markets and can often be discovered in rare ecclesiastical grandeur on church linens. Some handsome examples have been sighted in recent years in oddly diverse habitats, such as a gold-mine museum in the Transvaal, a horse-drawn caravan in southern Ireland and a heavy-goods vehicle on the island of Crete – shading the windscreen of the latter. The subject ranges from fine art to folk art.

Crochet is so much a part of the Victorian image that perhaps a gentle reminder will not be

Illust. 1 Camisole or chemise yoke, circa 1910. Edwardian yokes for undergarments were invariably front-fastened.

amiss that the bulk of surviving crochet is Edwardian, from the years 1901 to 1910, or even 'Georgian' referring to the following reign of George V.

A trend for the work was evident in England as early as the 1840s, and it had grown to become a fashionable cult by the 1880s and 1890s, but its undoubted heyday was the Edwardian era, when an infatuation with crochet reached almost manic proportions. It is usually assumed to have been a ladylike drawing-room pursuit of the well-to-do, but this concept is deceptive, for in fact a penchant for crochet crossed all strata of society and included the servant classes. Vast numbers became hookers – in the nicest sense of the word – for crochet is a French term meaning hook. Contemporary journals give the impression that women sat for hour upon hour plying their hooks with a dedicated stamina. No doubt fingers calloused at the task.

Illust. 2 Filet guipure crochet with an Art Nouveau influence. This was once an insertion in the centre of a cloth.

Too great an indulgence in crochet can be soporific, especially if the pattern is repetitive. Its therapeutic properties have always been well known, as shown by the following quotation[1] dating from circa 1916:

Of recent times medical authorities have declared that crochet work, undertaken in moderation, is one of the most beneficial of home hobbies, as it not only occupies the fingers, but the mind, and is soothing to the nerves. One eminent physician has gone so far as to recommend the pastime to men as well as to women, and to suggest that it might be regarded as a sedative and a substitute for a smoke.

Illust. 3 A table-cloth in plain filet crochet made in the 1940s.

Crochet is an easy work to lay aside and take up again, for there is only one implement, the hook, and only one stitch at a time, to be dropped in an emergency. It is thus an excellent occupation whilst travelling, which perhaps accounts for its former predilection among canal-boat and gypsy communities.

There is a natural division between the utilitarian wool crochet, which is comparable to knitting, and fine cotton crochet, which is comparable to lace. Few specimens of wool crochet have survived from earlier days, as usually these fell victim to hard wear or attack by moth. Most surviving examples, therefore, are of crochet lace. Even at the time of their making, many were considered as potential heirlooms or as acquisitions for a bottom drawer, and were cared for with a respect due to the hours spent on their execution, or to their intended future as trousseau lace.

The majority of the pieces featured in this book belong to the author, although some belong to Patricia Knowlden, who is an historian with an interest in crochet work. Further pieces from museum sources are acknowledged individually where necessary. The whole collection represents the work of many different women, known and unknown, but all now deceased.

A few flaws in workmanship are detectable to a critical eye, but these in no way detract from their value for study. Perhaps such imperfections should be noted with glee, for there is an oft-repeated fallacy that women were more generally skilled in days of yore, as though some common degeneracy had befallen us nowadays.

Of all the women who in one way or another have bequeathed their work, only a few can be identified with certainty, and the following notes are included as much for social interest as for a record of their achievements.

Miss Daisy Bird, of Streatham, was a school teacher who meticulously documented anything of potential interest to her pupils. Her major contribution is a sample book which she assembled during the years 1910 to 1913, and which proclaims *The 'Balmoral' Needlework Book for Children's Specimens* on its cover.

Mrs Jessie Maud Gedye, also of South London, was a crochet devotee with an instinctive judgement for beautiful design, who learnt to crochet as a nursery maid at about 14 years of age, circa 1911. Luckily, she had a tendency to begin ambitious pieces of work and then run out of thread, or of impetus, leaving them unfinished, which prevented them from ever being used. This has ensured their survival, and it is a heartening thought to those of us who leave unfinished projects languishing in our cupboards, that the items we never complete can be of more use to posterity than the work we actually finish.

Mrs Nellie Knowlden, of Rothwell, near Leeds, was a talented craftswoman, justly proud of the fact that prior to her marriage in 1916 she had risen regularly at six in the morning to work on additions to her bottom drawer. Several of her laces are featured here, but her greatest contribution has been the series of crochet

Illust. 4 Doyley with 'shells' of chain loops. The pattern is ➤
from Needlecraft, *No. 41, 1908.*

journals which she preserved, and which have yielded a great deal of historic information.

Mrs Kate Laker, of the village of Cerne Abbas in Dorset, learnt to crochet at a dame school in the 1890s, and was later apprenticed to a milliner. She married comparatively late in life, by which time the garments set aside earlier for her trousseau had become out of date. They were left in storage, undisturbed, until the 1940s, when her nieces fell on this hoard, ravaged the petticoats and nightgowns and wore the crochet-edged camisoles as summer blouses. Kate's unwanted tableware survived the onslaught and is included here.

Mrs Margaret Elizabeth Short, also of Cerne Abbas, began her working life as a lady's maid, and was taught to crochet in the mid-1880s by her mother who had come from Ireland. Both were well steeped in the art of Irish crochet, and although very little of their work has been spared, their hooks are shown.

Doyleys, which abound in so many varieties in any accumulation of old crochet, first appeared as round dessert napkins in the early eighteenth century. Doyley (with all its various spellings) was the name of a famous London haberdasher.

Illust. 5 This doyley design is more complex than it appears to be. The circular motifs are not completed individually but each wanders across the 'ground' of its neighbour.

PART ONE
HISTORICAL ANALYSIS

1

HISTORICAL DEVELOPMENT OF TECHNIQUE

Crochet and knitting are so interrelated that they are usually assumed to have had a common origin. There is a cross between the two, called Tunisian crochet (discussed in chapter 4) which may well have been that origin, for it is a method where stitches are held in a row on a long hooked needle. Hand-knitting once went through a stage when it was worked on a pair of hooked needles, and any inquisitive knitter in search of enlightenment is recommended to try it. Progress is slow but stitches do not drop.

Heinz Edgar Kiewe, in his book, *The Sacred History of Knitting*[1], also remarks on the sacred history of crochet, and suggests that it was practised in the Near East before the days of Solomon. This may well be an over estimate, but it is generally accepted that both crochet and knitting evolved in the early Arabic civilisations, from whence they spread with the exodus of Arab traders. Authorities differ slightly on dates, but the earliest knitted fragments discovered in archeological excavations are from the second to seventh centuries AD. The earliest written reference to crochet hooks, quoted by Kiewe, is dated between the years AD 50 to 137.

There is also a theory that the crafts developed elsewhere as a parallel and independent growth. Kristin Bühler, writing in *Ciba Review*[2], gives an account of ethnic studies among the Warrau Indians of Venezuela, and points out that their techniques of crochet and knitting differ so widely from any other known methods that their knowledge could not have been acquired from an outside source.

Obviously, some simple form of wool crochet has been known for a long time. One can only guess at the stitches used; probably they were chain stitch, slip stitch, double crochet and Tunisian crochet, all of which give a close-textured and protective fabric. Such crochet occurs, often in vivid colour contrasts, in peasant and tribal communities all over the world. There has always been a strong tradition of crochet among Muslim populations of the Middle East, and it is evident also in tribal cultures of central and northern Africa (as the name Tunisian implies).

Crochet as lace was a European development which began to make an appearance as metallic chain lace in the sixteenth century. The wardrobe accounts of Queen Elizabeth I, dated 1580, include a 'gowne . . . layed aboute with vj small cheyne laces of gold', and an inventory of Kenilworth Castle dated 1588 describes beds 'garnished with a chaine lace of goulde and silver-copper'[3].

Illust. 6 shows an example of late seventeenth-century chain lace[4]. It is four inches in width, and made entirely of crochet chains, connected with slip stitch. The full length of the lace has a repeating pattern, and there is a definite right and wrong side, which suggests that it was worked on a parchment foundation on to which the design was drawn. Outline chains were apparently laid first and tacked to the foundation, then filling chains were freely worked

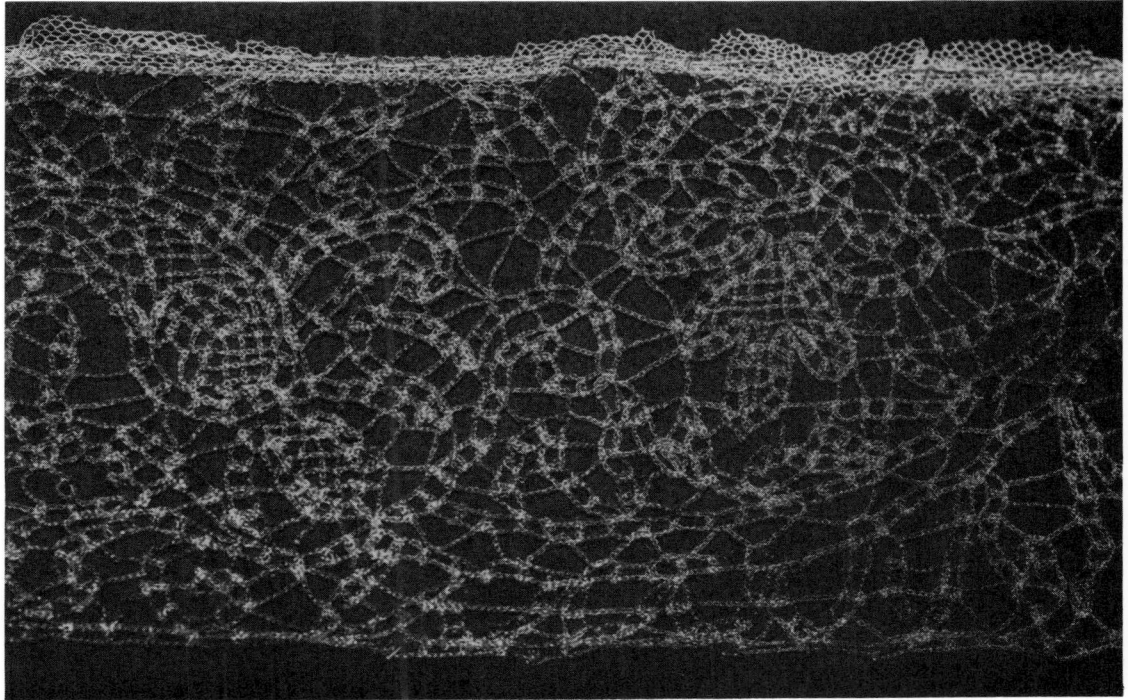

Illust. 6 Late seventeenth-century chain lace. Victoria and Albert Museum.

to and from the outline, often crossing over each other. The finished portion would then have been removed from its foundation and the latter prepared for the next repeat. Despite the vague nature of the design, the lace is a remarkable example of chain lace. It shows no sign of having been worked with a needle, although it may well have been made on a revolving bolster pillow, which was the usual method for making needlepoint laces.

Further wardrobe accounts of Elizabeth I include 'six caules of Knot-work worked with chainstitch and bound with tape, of nun's thread'[5], i.e., of fine lace thread. This could of course be interpreted as netting, 'worked' or embroidered with chain stitch, but taken at face value, it is an accurate description of crochet net.

There are several further references to chain lace in sixteenth-century wills and inventories[6],

and an interesting later reference occurs in a bill dated 1772 from an upholsterer's in Clerkenwell and Cornhill, which lists '86 yds white Thread chain lace at $2\frac{1}{2}$d . . . for bed cover and hangings, and a further 30 yards for curtains'[7].

There is strong evidence to suggest that tambour work influenced a wider outbreak of crochet lace. Tambouring had been introduced into Europe from the Far East, and was well established by the middle of the eighteenth century. It consisted of chain stitch worked on the surface of a loosely woven muslin with the aid of a fine hook. Machine-made nets later replaced the muslin.

Bone or ivory tambour hooks were ornately carved and nearly always had a screw fitting at the side of the handle to hold a removable steel hook in place. Several different sizes of hook could be stored in the end of a detachable handle. In use a tambour hook is held vertically. Crochet hooks are held horizontally, in a totally different grip, and any ornament or screw-fitting is detrimental to speed in crochet and will make the

Fig. 1 A tambour hook.

hand sore. Nevertheless, tambour hooks were apparently used for crochet work.

An advertisement in *Six Square Doyleys in Crochet*, edited by George Curling Hope in 1848 states

The editor begs to announce that he has invented and registered a new Tambour Handle and Needles, as an improvement on those now in use for Crochet Work, by obviating the necessity of the unsightly screw at the side.

Hooks were classed as needles until well into the present century. Early pattern books frequently referred to slip stitch as 'tambour stitch'.

In 1840, Mrs Jane Gaugain of Edinburgh published *The Lady's Assistant for executing useful and fancy designs in Knitting, Netting and Crochetwork*, using the terms 'single tambour' to describe slip stitch, 'French tambour' and 'double tambour' to describe double crochet, and 'open tambour' to describe a treble followed by a chain.

Tambouring was known as crochet in France, and by the latter end of the eighteenth century a technique of working *crochet en l'air* was common. 'Crochet in the air', without the support of a muslin backing, was not a new art, but it was treated as such and acquired a ladylike acceptability. It had become a fashionable drawing room pursuit. The French term for a chain is still *mailles en l'air*, literally 'stitches in the air'.

In 1842, Miss Frances Lambert writing in *The Handbook of Needlework*, says

Crochet work, although long known and practised, did not attract particular attention until within the last four years since which time it has been brought to great perfection, and has been applied with success to the production of numerous ornamental works.

Following Miss Lambert, *Weldon's Practical Needlework*, Vol. 1, 1886, offers

Crochet, or, as it was called by the Scotch, "shepherd's knitting", has really only been practised during the last half century, and in fact barely that, for it was about 1838 that it became publicly known in Great Britain, for, although it dates back from the 16th century, it was then called "nun's work" simply because it was only known to the nuns, who made lovely laces and different articles.

The term 'shepherd's knitting', which evokes an arcadian image of Little Bo Peep denuding her flock, is more appropriate to Tunisian crochet, but it seems to have been loosely applied to any simple form of wool crochet[8].

Illust. 7 Patterns depending on the treble stitch.

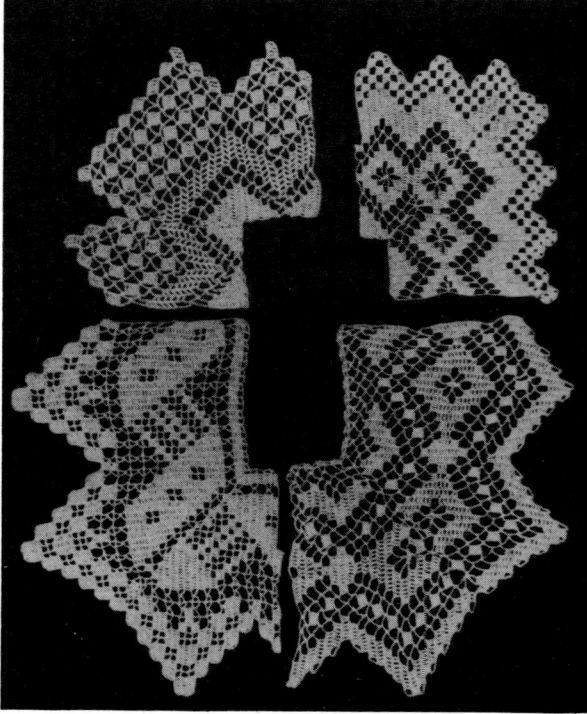

Illust. 8 A cuff showing a beautiful combination of grouped and interlinked stitch arrangements.

The treble stitch appears to have evolved at about the end of the eighteenth century. Perhaps it was an accidental discovery, made by a careless worker in a dim light allowing her thread to tangle on the hook, as thread is so apt to do, yet having the foresight to realise the potential advantage of a longer stitch. Once the long stitch, the treble, had become an accepted practice, then the double and triple trebles would have followed very quickly, as they are all dependent on the same principal. It was an important development, for a whole new range of complicated stitch arrangements were then feasible. Stitches could be combined, divided, pierced, padded, picoted and interlinked in all sorts of creative ways.

Not everyone was enthusiastic. George Eliot[9], writing in the 1850s, had a slightly jaundiced view as she wrote

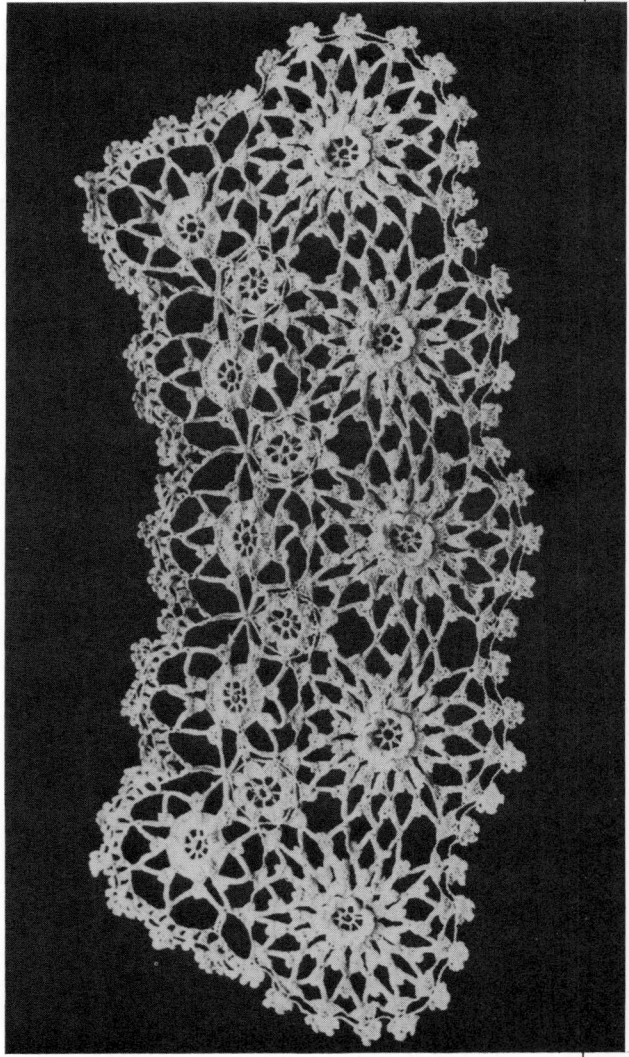

When a man is happy enough to win the affections of a sweet girl who can soothe his cares with crochet, and respond to all his most cherished ideas with beaded urn-rugs and chair-covers in German wool, he has, at least, a guarantee of domestic comfort, whatever trials may await him out of doors. What a resource it is under fatigue and irritation to have your drawing-room well supplied with small mats, which would always be ready if you ever wanted to set anything upon them! And what styptic for a bleeding heart can equal copious squares of crochet . . .

2
HISTORICAL DEVELOPMENT OF DESIGN

Traditionally, wool crochet designs were based on stitch permutations, such as the many variations of the shell shawl patterns, and the treble block patterns. These were formations which a worker could devise for herself by counting stitches and spaces, either singly or in groups, and even though, in some cases interchange of these elements could result in exceedingly complex patterns, they were easily worked by eye.

Lace crochet designs do not seem to have evolved in this way at all. Many were deliberate attempts to copy existing needlepoint and bobbin laces, and to produce them at a speed faster than needlepoint or bobbin techniques would allow, for crochet was, and still is, a comparatively quick method of lace-making. Some were faithful copies of these laces, or as faithful a copy as is possible with the use of a hook. Others were less exact reproductions, the original being a source of inspiration rather than a model.

It is well known that Irish crochet (discussed in chapter 3) was based on the wonderful Venetian point laces, and it is a reasonable assumption from its appearance that filet crochet (discussed in chapter 4) was based on the true filet lace or lacis, but other types of lace were copied too. *Weldon's Practical Needlework*, Vol 17, No. 197, published in 1902, offers 'Fine Torchon Lace', 'Torchon Lace with Tufts', 'Torchon Lace for Bedspread', 'Torchon Lace for Traycloth', 'Torchon Lace for Underlinen', all of these being crochet designs!

Of all the bobbin laces, torchon, with its diamond-shaped ground or net as a characteristic feature, is probably the easiest to transform into crochet. Illust. 9 shows a true torchon lace made with bobbins, and for comparison, Illust. 10 shows torchon crochet, the latter being a very obvious copy. It imitates the fans, trails, ground, and even the foot of the

Illust. 9 Torchon lace.

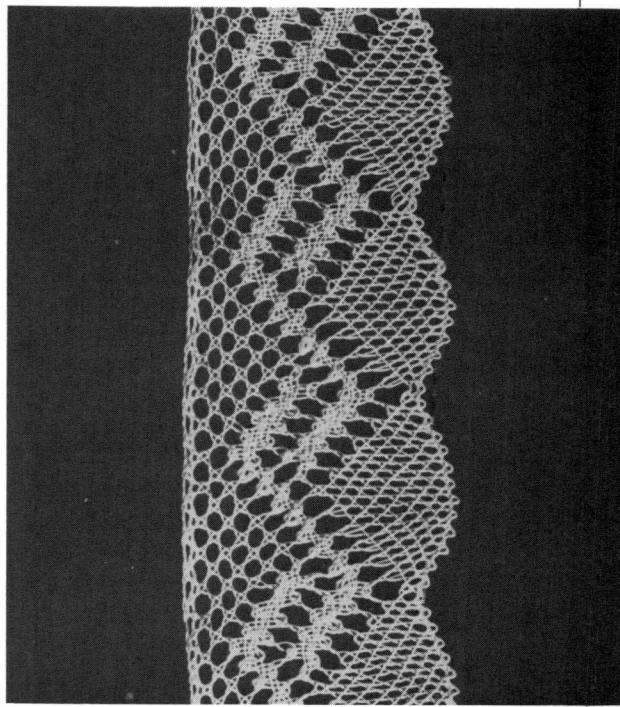

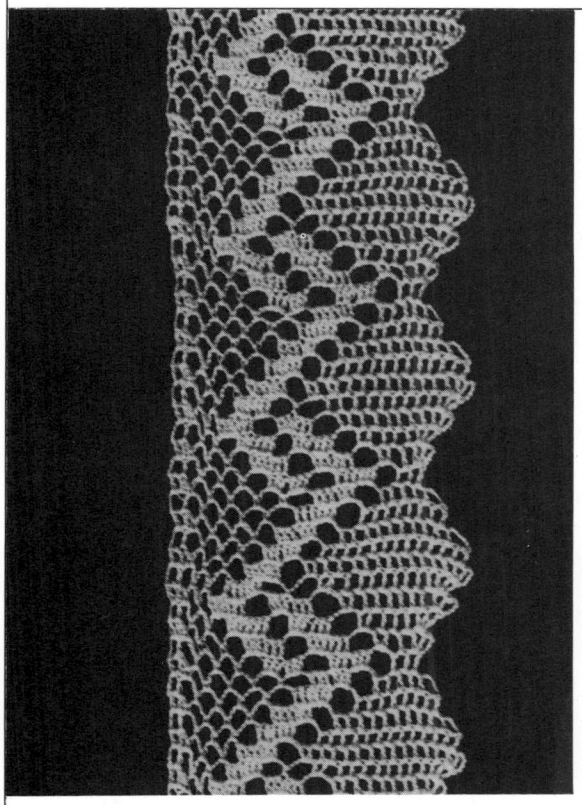

Illust. 10 Torchon crochet. *Illust. 11 Cluny lace.* ➤

Illust. 12 Cluny crochet. ➤

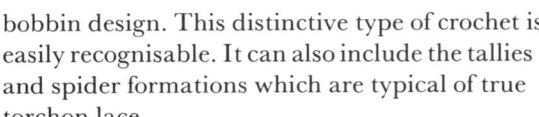

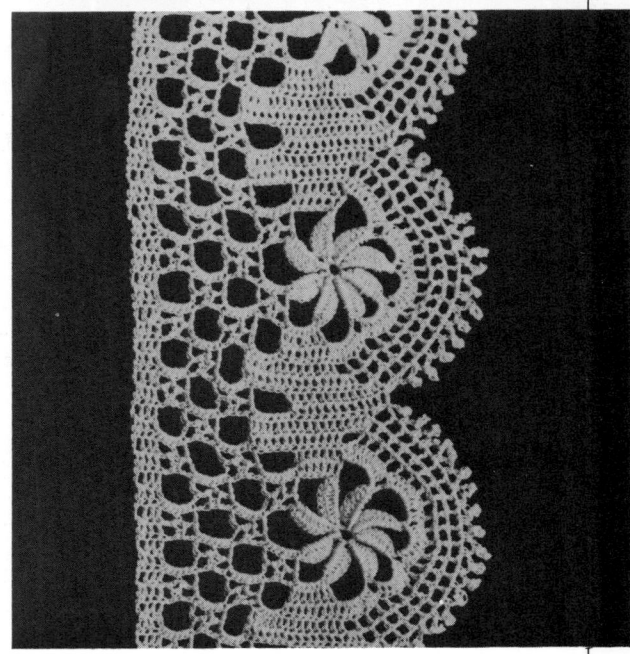

bobbin design. This distinctive type of crochet is easily recognisable. It can also include the tallies and spider formations which are typical of true torchon lace.

Fancy Needlework Illustrated, No. 11, 1909, gives a pattern for 'Crochet Torchon Lace and Corner' which is a reasonable copy of a 'Cluny Edging' from Margaret Maidment's *Manual of Handmade Bobbin Lacework*.[1] Cluny and torchon are often confused in theory and mixed in practice. Illust. 11 shows the bobbin lace in question, and Illust. 12 shows the crochet.

Fancy Needlework Illustrated, No. 23, 1912, gives a pattern, 'Cluny Crochet Lace and Insertion with Corner', stating, 'This charming crochet pattern was adapted from a valuable piece of

HERITAGE CROCHET: AN ANALYSIS

Cluny Lace'. *Crochet Book*, by Mlle Riego, 18th Series, 1856, contains edgings and borders in 'Cluny Laces' and 'Maltese Laces'.

Maltese crochet was also a counterpart of bobbin lace. Any pattern which included a ground of the little leaf-shaped tallies so characteristic of Maltese bobbin lace was called Maltese crochet.

In *The Point-Lace Crochet Collar Book*, 1846, Mrs Warren maintains that her patterns 'closely resemble the rare and valuable Old Point and

Illust. 13 Maltese crochet.

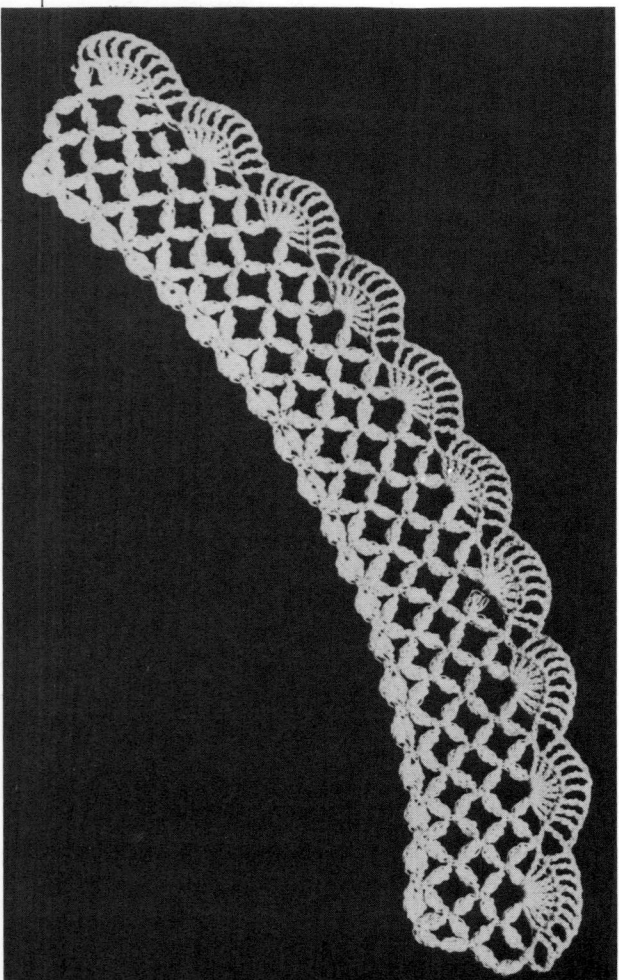

Illust. 14 Parasol cover in Honiton crochet, 1892. Victoria and ➤ *Albert Museum.*

Mechlin laces', and there is a reference to Honiton crochet in *Fancy Needlework Illustrated*, No. 1, 1907. *Crochet Book*, by Mlle Riego, 5th series, 1849, includes a pattern for a 'Crochet Honiton Collar' made of tiny sprigs applied to Brussels net. Honiton crochet is also featured by Flora Klickmann in her series of *Home Art* books. The term may well surprise Honiton lace-makers, but it was a name applied in general to floral and leaf sprigs made somewhat in the traditions of fine Irish crochet but devoid of raised or padded work. The sprigs were sometimes connected with needlepoint or crochet bars, and sometimes mounted on net.

Needlepoint laces were often easy to copy because double crochet stitches, tightly worked over a chain, closely resemble the buttonhole bars of needlepoint techniques. Some simple little edgings of chain loops covered with double crochet are given in *Needlecraft Practical Journal*, No. 58, 1911, and the editor announces, 'We are pleased to be able to include some Hedebo Crochet Edgings. It will be found on comparing these little edgings with the needle worked laces . . . that they are an exact imitation of the real Hedebo lace; the great advantage of the crochet being that it is worked much more quickly. If linen thread is used, detection is almost impossible'.

Fancy Needlework Illustrated, No. 23, 1912,

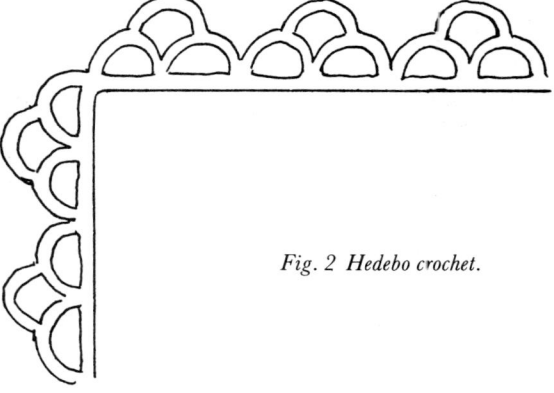

Fig. 2 Hedebo crochet.

unwittingly a rich source of information, gives 'Crochet Edging, Reticella Pattern', and states, 'This is an excellent reproduction in crochet of a specimen of the beautiful "Reticella" lace that Vandyke loved to depict'. Another issue of the same journal gives a pattern for 'Reticella Crochet Medallions . . . done in imitation of a section of beautiful Reticella lace'.

HERITAGE CROCHET: AN ANALYSIS

Illust. 15 Reticella crochet.

derivative. There are certain naturally occurring formations resulting from the need for ever-enlarging increases in circular work, which are sufficiently alluring in themselves to form the basis of 'designer crochet'. Success usually depends on strict adherence to a regular mathematical formula.

A classic example is the phenomenon in which side-stepped increases result in a 'whirlpool' effect, as shown in Illusts 16 and 76. This effect is a feature of considerable potential interest for designers, and it has been used again and again in different guises.

Illust. 16 A 'whirlpool'.

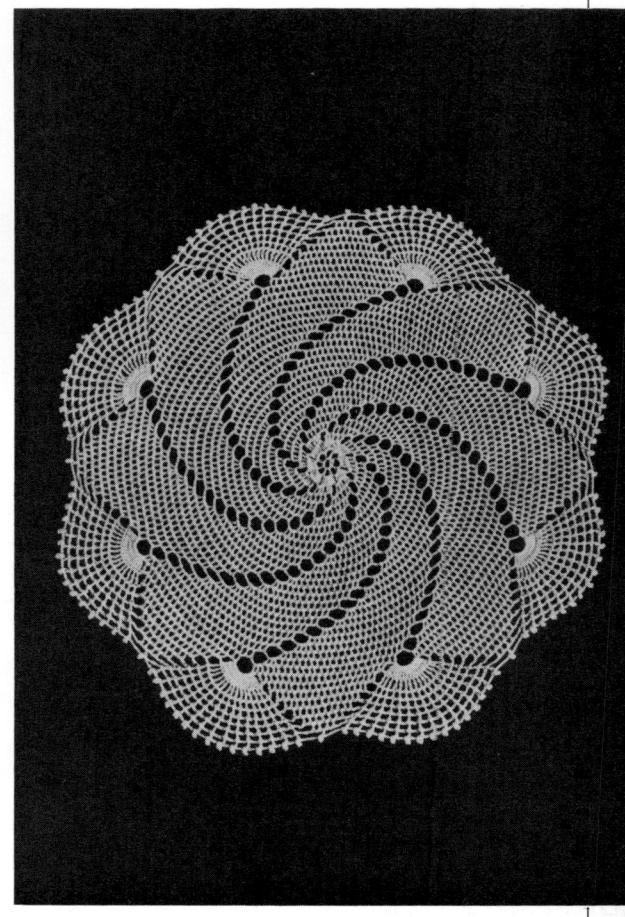

Reticella, literally 'little net', was an Italian needlepoint, also called Italian or Greek Point, which began as a cutwork embroidery on linen, and later developed into *punto in aria* or 'stitch in air', without a fabric base, but still retaining the geometric character of the original cutwork. It enjoyed a revival as 'Ruskin Lace' during the 1880s in the Lake District.

Sometimes it is possible to trace the influence of more than one type of lace in a crochet design, for sources became confused. It is not unusual to find a pastiche of torchon and filet in the same piece, an impossibility where the true laces are concerned, but perfectly feasible with a crochet technique.

However, the old designs were not entirely

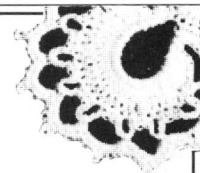

3
IRISH CROCHET

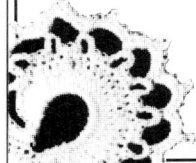

The magnificent Irish crochet laces can be divided into two groups according to their construction. The Irish guipures (guipures d'Irlande) also known as Irish Point, where sprigs are made individually and afterwards assembled, form one group, and the Irish baby (Bébé) laces, where motif and ground are worked as one, form the other.

Illust. 17 Collar in Irish guipure, circa 1850.

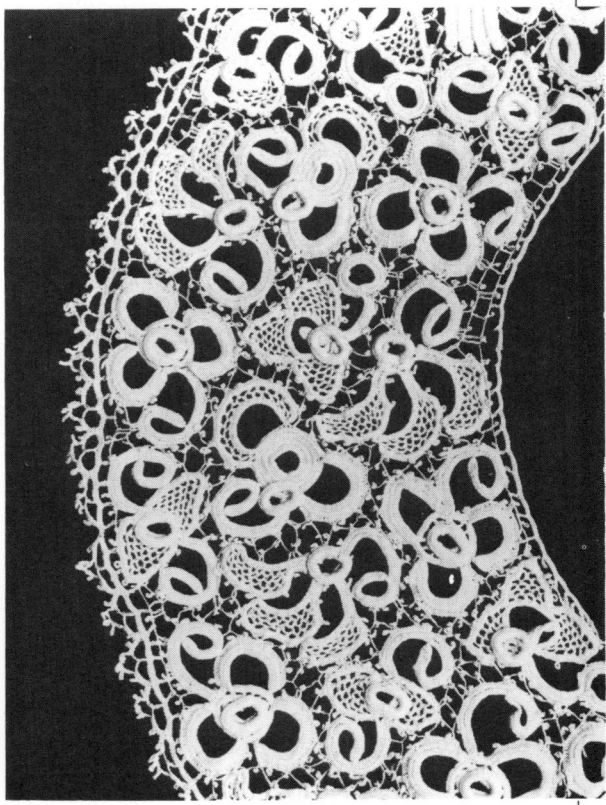

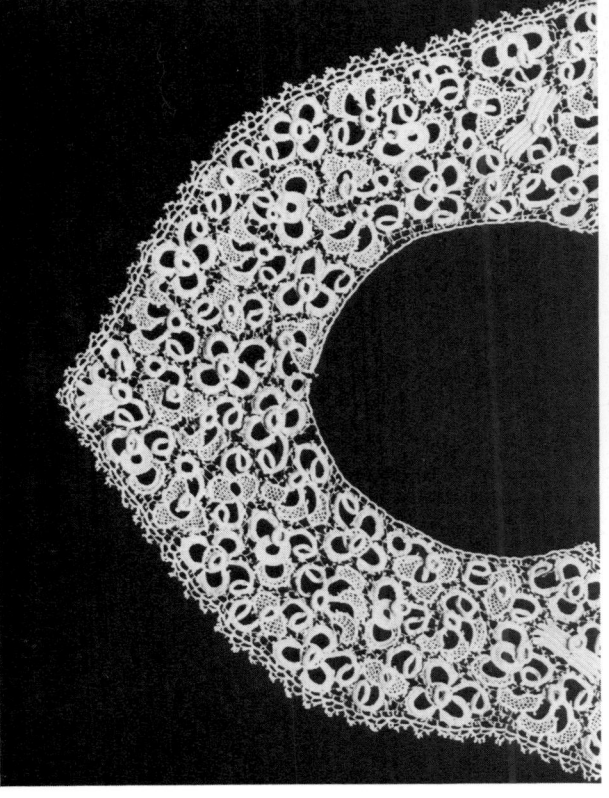

Illust. 18 Close-up of Illust. 17. The small padded rings were sewn into place afterwards.

The guipures are also distinguished by their heavy padding, achieved by working over a cord, whereas the baby laces are not padded, although the rose and shamrock motifs which so typify this

Illust. 19 Irish baby crochet, showing a typical rose and shamrock motif and picot mesh.

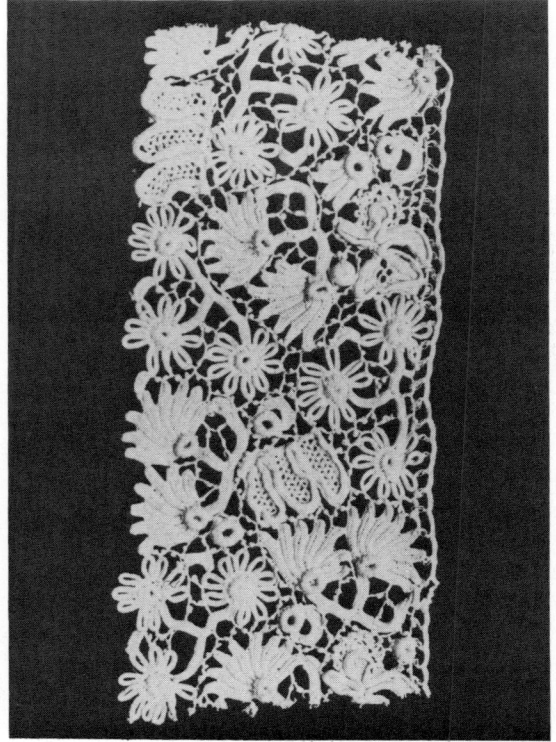

Illust. 20 Irish guipure, circa 1850.

Illust. 21 A close up of Illust. 20. The knotted picots were known as Clones knots.

group are generally formed of superimposed layers, which create a raised surface without the aid of padding.

Few cottage industries can have a more interesting or better documented history than that of Irish crochet, and it has been thoroughly researched by Ada Longfield[1] and Elizabeth Boyle[2]. It developed in an Ursuline Convent School founded by French-educated nuns in Blackrock, County Cork, in the late-eighteenth century, but only began to flourish as a viable enterprise in 1845, when the school received the sum of £90 for crochet made by the children.

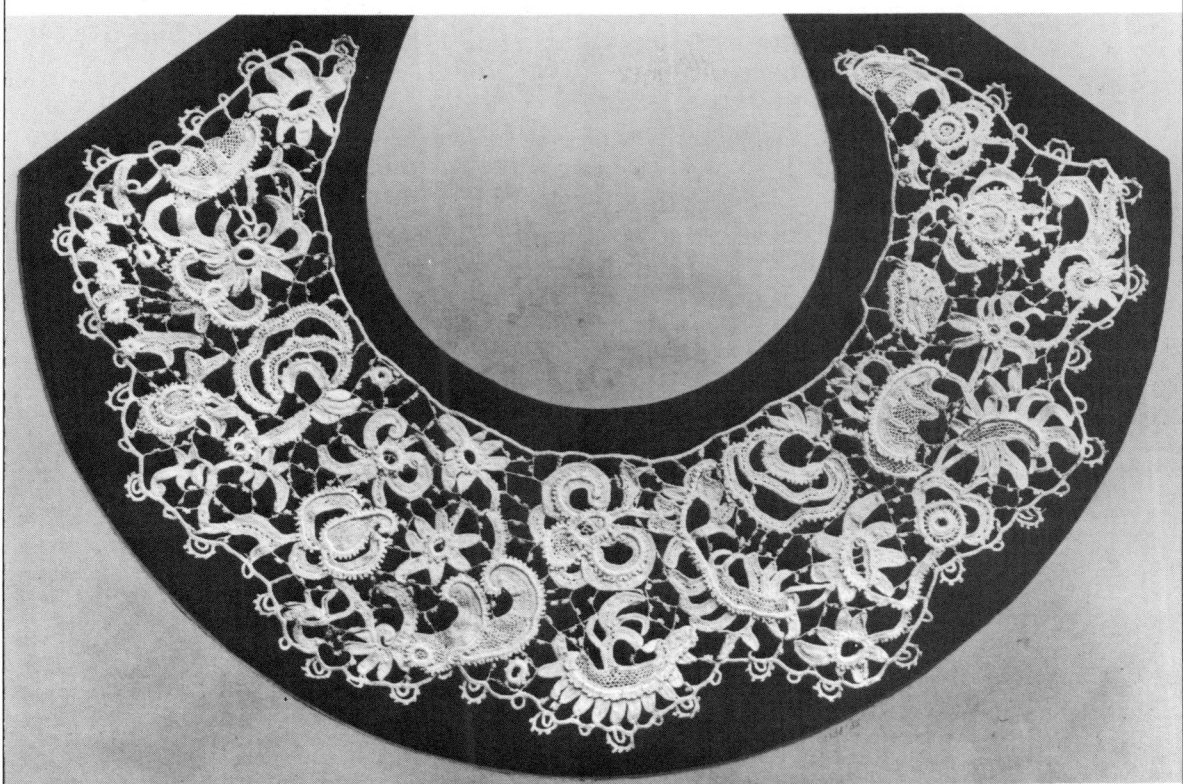

Illust. 22 Collar of Irish guipure, 1855. Victoria and Albert Museum.

During the dreadful famine years of the late 1840s, further convent orders, notably those at Youghal, Kinsale and Tralee, devoted themselves to the teaching and marketing of crochet on a commercial basis, and to this end also Mrs Susannah Meredith started the Adelaide Industrial School in Cork in 1847. Their ventures met with such wild success that at one time 12,000 women and children in the neighbourhood of Cork alone were employed with their hooks[3]. These were invariably home-made contrivances of wire inserted into a wooden handle. The threads used at this time were relatively cheap cottons, and sample books were in common use since many workers found difficulty in understanding written instructions, but could follow ready-made pieces by eye. Stitches were seldom counted.

Labour was organized on the classic 'putting-out' system, and several workers would be engaged in the production of a single piece. The basic sprigs were made at home, then delivered to a central workroom where others would do attachment work – tack the sprigs face downwards on to tough brown paper or glazed calico on which the laces were planned, and lay-in the filling threads or ground.

Crochet played an important part in relieving the distress prevalent in Ireland during the famine years. Large numbers of emigrants were known to have saved enough from the work to pay for a passage to America, and Mrs Meredith of the Adelaide School relates that a certain child, by her toil, was able to free her mother and sister from residence in a workhouse.

Further north, Clones, in County Monaghan,

became famed under the management of Mrs Cassandra Hands, wife of the rector of Clones. So wretched was existence in this area that even men and boys were glad to work at crochet. Clones was renowned for the outstanding quality of its workmanship and design. Division of labour was not usual here. The Clones designs were inspired by Venetian Gros Point and Rose Point, the most prized of the old Venetian needlepoint laces.

These imitations of Venetian needlepoints were loosely-termed Venetian crochet. There were several minor variants, now difficult to identify, such as Jesuit crochet and Spanish crochet, which acquired their names from needlepoint laces owned by various Spanish religious houses, and later procured by Irish convents.

As the famine receded, impetus slackened. Standards of communal work were always

difficult to monitor, and variations became too apparent, to the general detriment of the whole. Trade had so diminished by 1860 that the Blackrock, Youghal and Kinsale Convent Schools and the Adelaide Industrial School were forced to cease production.

By the 1880s there were signs of an overall revival. Heavy laces were again in fashion, and perhaps the gradual invasion of machine-made copies and of 'Irish crochet' imports from the Far East may have promoted a reaction. Irish teachers were offered the opportunity of art school study, with the result that designs vastly improved. Linen threads came into general use, and there were improved sales facilities, such as

Illust. 23 Little Lord Fauntleroy *collar in Irish guipure, circa 1890. The fashion for this type of collar followed from Frances Hodgson Burnett's book of the same name, published in 1886.*

Illust. 24 A close-up of Illust. 23.

those provided by the Irish Industries Association, whence Queen Victoria and the Princess of Wales were known to have purchased Irish crochet[4].

By the 1890s success had echoed well beyond Ireland. Guipure d'Irlande and the Bébé laces were renowned in fashionable stores in London, New York and Paris, for the French couturiers, Paquin especially, lavished it on their gowns. The advent of the opulent Edwardian era marked a peak for its revival, and as the making of Irish crochet progressed from a cottage industry to a popular drawing-room pastime, a more sophisticated approach was deemed necessary.

Weldon's Practical Needlework devoted issues Nos 182, 186, 188, 215 and 351, published between 1901 and 1915, entirely to Irish crochet, and the Northern School of Art Needlework in Manchester, (publishers of *Fancy Needlework Illustrated*) produced a superb manual, *Irish Crochet Lace: A Handbook of Practical Instruction*, circa 1914. Dollfus-Mieg et Cie, (D.M.C.), of France, published *La Guipure d'Irlande*, which included patterns ready-traced on glazed calico, in 1910, and the Priscilla Publishing Co., of Boston, introduced the Priscilla *Irish Crochet*, Books 1 and 2, circa 1909.

Needlecraft Practical Journal devoted Nos 21, 27, 43 and 80, issued between 1905 and 1914, entirely to Irish crochet. A general introduction to No. 21 includes the following;

Irish crochet lace is a most fascinating work to those who have a good eye for form, and who like a certain freedom in the arrangement of designs. In working the sprigs or objects the cord padding is an important factor, for by its tightness or slackness, stems or leaves of the various designs can be artistically curved in any direction desired, and it can give an appearance of life

Illust. 25 A cuff matching the Little Lord Fauntleroy *collar.*

Fig. 4 Boudoir shoe covered in Irish crochet, 1914.

Fig. 3 Hook used for Irish crochet, 1905.

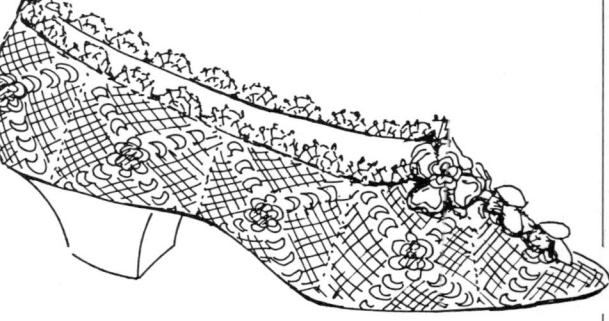

to the leaf or flower which the usual counted stitches alone can never give. For this reason the directions for a sprig may be carefully followed by two workers, and yet the two may turn out quite different results.

An ominous little warning follows

There are few kinds of work to beat Irish crochet lace for its facility for getting in a hopeless state of confusion.

A dumpy cork-handled hook was preferred, and gauges, for sizing the tiny rings which were the basis for the majority of the sprigs, were made from broken pieces of knitting needle.

An 'Emerald Foundation', marketed under the Penelope trade mark, was designed for use with the sprigs given in *Needlecraft Practical Journal*. As the name implies, it was a green-coloured fabric sufficiently tough for hard use, for once the sprigs were tacked into position the foundation needed to be continually folded back out of the way in order to allow room for manipulation of the hook when working the ground.

IRISH CROCHET

Illust. 26 The Trefoil *motif.*

The following directions for a trefoil, shown much enlarged in Illust. 26 are given in order to demonstrate how the padding cord was manipulated in making Irish guipure.

TREFOIL, from *Needlecraft Practical Journal*, No. 27, 1906

Take 4 strands of padding thread, work over the cord thus formed 48 doubles and join to form a ring, and draw in closely.
2nd Round: Work treble stitch over the cord into each stitch of the centre ring.
3rd Round: ** 12 double over the cord into the first 12 stitches of last round; 8 chain join to eighth of the last 12 double; 1 double, 15 treble, 1 double under the 8 chain; 4 double over the cord into the next 4 stitches of last round, 1 double over the cord alone to turn it, 20 treble over the cord, 1 treble over the cord into the centre stitch of the last 15 treble, 20 treble, 1 double over the cord, join to the fourth of the last 12 double, turn, 4 double over the cord into the back strands of the next 4 treble, * 5 chain, 1 double over the cord into the same stitch as the last double, 3 double over the cord into the back strands of the next

3 treble; repeat from * till you come to the second round again. Repeat from ** twice more; finish the trefoil with 4 double over the cord into the next 4 stitches and fasten off. For the centre wind the padding thread 25 times round the tip of your forefinger and work double stitches closely round this ring, edge the ring as follows: * 7 chain, miss 3, 1 double into the fourth stitch. Repeat from * all round. Sew this firmly on the centre of the trefoil. These rings are best added the last thing when the filling has been worked and the crochet removed from the cambric foundation.

There was a considerable spin-off from Irish

Illust. 27 'Irish crochet' from India, early twentieth century. At least four different women were involved, judging by the variations in workmanship.

◄ Illust. 28 More 'Irish crochet' from India, early twentieth century. Notice the double layered shamrocks.

Illust. 29 An 'Irish' derivative from Shanghai, early twentieth century.

crochet. Copycat industries, also activated by poverty, gradually emerged in China and in India, all organised on similar 'putting-out' systems. Legend tells that the Indian crochet lace industry, centred at Narsapur (also known as Narasapur), on the coast of Andhra Pradesh, resulted from the teaching of Irish nuns shipwrecked off the coast, circa 1860. However, a conflicting version suggests that missionary wives had preceded these efforts at the Godavari Delta mission school in the 1840s or 50s[5].

At first the produce was sent to Ireland for sale, but by 1900 exports were being organised on a wider and more efficient commercial scale. The Indian industry expanded further in the 1920s, exporting widely to all the British dominions, to Europe, USA and South America.

Over the years the work gradually lost its Irish character, although vestiges of its ancestry remain still.

Industrial work from the Far East can often be identified by its looseness, for workers economise on thread in this way. Large pieces often betray signs of communal workmanship, and since speed is a great factor in earning a living at crochet work, ends of thread are seldom properly finished.

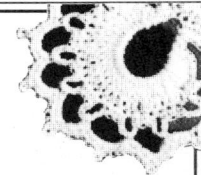

4
MORE TYPES OF CROCHET

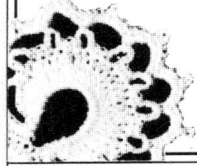

A name may refer to a place of origin, special technique, design, stitch or thread. *Sobritto crochet*, common in the 1930s and 40s, owes its name to a rayon thread, while *Pineapple crochet* and *Wheat-ear crochet* (see Illust. 83) refer to particular types of design. *Greek crochet* may not necessarily be crochet from Greece, for it was a name given in the past to reticella designs.

Illust. 30 Pineapple crochet, circa 1916.

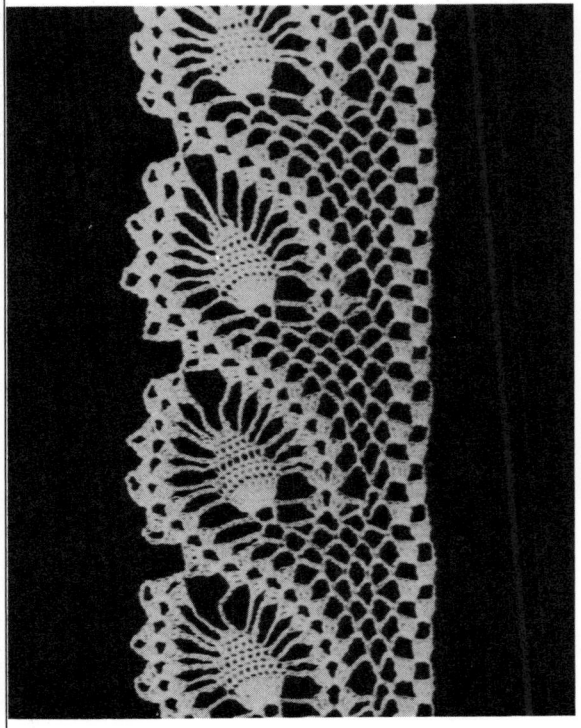

Illust. 31 Plain filet crochet, circa 1918.

A deceptive Irish relationship can be seen in Spanish and Italian work. The beautiful *Orvieto crochet*[1] from Italy, has an apparent Irish

Illust. 32 Yoke in plain filet crochet, 1920s.

Illust. 33 Primrose design in filet guipure crochet measuring eight inches in depth.

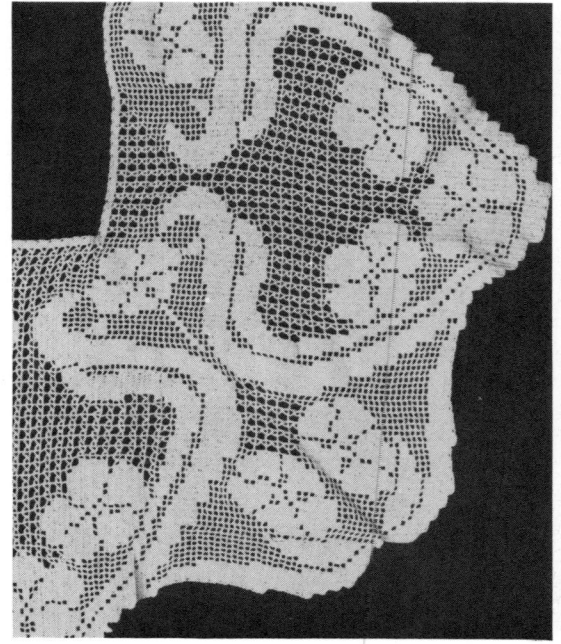

derivation, till one remembers that the Irish designs were based on old Venetian needlepoint laces, and then it is obvious that the Orvieto work derives at first-hand from the Venetian needlepoints, and is a 'sister' to Irish crochet. With the famed Italian flair for design, Orvieto crochet is outstanding in this respect, for its designs were inspired originally by carvings in the Orvieto Cathedral. Similarly, *Azores crochet*[2] belongs to the same Irish sisterhood.

Filet crochet developed from filet lace, or lacis, which is of very old origin. Filet lace is traditionally needle-darned on a square-meshed net, and the ever-apparent square grid is its distinguishing characteristic. The manufacture of machine nets in the nineteenth century led to a widening of interest in the subject, under such names as Filet Guipure, Guipure d'Art and Filet Richelieu, where nets were not so much darned

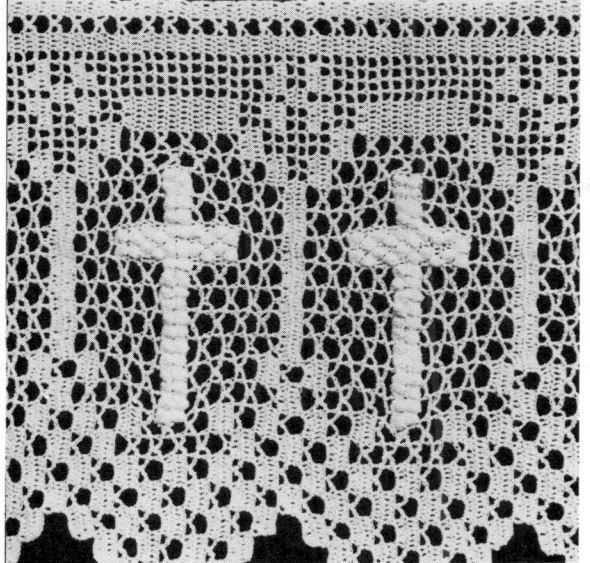

Illust. 34 Filet guipure crochet Cathedral lace, *with tufted trebles. The design is from* Fancy Needlework Illustrated, *No. 33, 1915.*

Illust. 35 Shadow crochet. The design is from Weldon's Practical Needlework, *No. 321, 1912.*

as embossed with elaborate embroidered fillings. The wider range of these laces, led in turn to a wider range of filet crochet derivatives.

Plain filet crochet has a square net formed by working two chain stitches between trebles, with solid blocks of treble corresponding to the darned blocks of true filet lace. There is a more ornate filet crochet, corresponding to filet guipure, which has more variety in design. The most common variation is the lacet net. Filet crochet executed on a larger scale, using double trebles to replace the usual trebles, is now called *Lacis crochet*.

From time to time, fashions recur for treating crochet net as if it were machine- or hand-made net, adding darning or embroidery. These styles are usually given a straightforward descriptive name such as *Darned crochet*. The net of plain filet crochet is also used as a basis for mock 'tambouring', adding not only chain stitch but also double crochet or treble stitches, so that these stand on the surface. As might be expected, the technique is called *Tambour crochet* or *Surface crochet*. Surface crochet can also be worked on a more solid crochet background, and is a technique used in the relatively new *Aran crochet*, so called because it imitates Aran knitting.

Shadow crochet or *Triolet crochet*[3] is related to both filet and torchon crochet. The designs are not always clearly defined, hence the suggestion of shadow. The net has a three-sided mesh, and solid areas are of treble shells.

Gros crochet is a coarse furnishing crochet of sprigs applied to crochet net. The net varies in

Fig. 5 Some braids used in conjunction with crochet. A, Rice or Coronation braid; B, Mignardise braid; C, fancy lace braid.

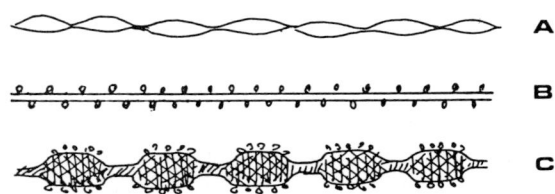

character, and often the sprigs are sewn to the net after making.

Braided crochet has been a recurrent fashion since mid-Victorian times. There are two types; the braid itself can be pre-worked in crochet, or a machine-made braid can be used. For the latter, there was formerly a wide range of choice available, such as imitation Honiton lace braids, picot-edged Mignardise braids, and Rice or Coronation braids, which were glossy indented cords, useful for folding into petal formations. The crochet braids ranged from fine hairpin work to heavy corded efforts resembling macramé cords. Not surprisingly designs featuring the latter were termed *Macramé crochet*. Confusingly, macramé crochet was also a name used for any sturdy crochet worked in macramé thread.

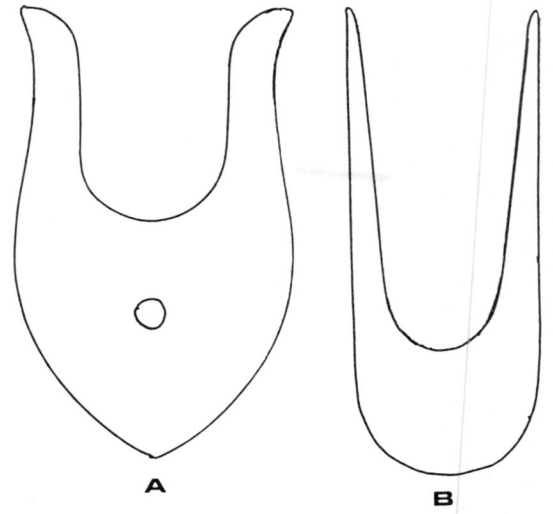

Fig. 6 A, a lucet (the cord is pulled through the central hole); B, a hairpin fork.

technique may have evolved from a fork known as a lucet (or lucette) which was in general use till the end of the eighteenth century for cord making[4]. For this purpose, the lucet was continually turned from side to side in the hand, and the same method is characteristic of hairpin crochet. The braids are worked with either a double crochet or treble, repeated vertically, the hairpin being turned sideways at every repeat so

Fig. 7 Peacock's Eye or broomstick crochet.

Illust. 36 A doyley edged with hairpin crochet.

Hairpin crochet, quaintly described as *Krotchee* in Victorian publications, is a braid made in conjunction with a hairpin or similar two-pronged fork. Early forms were made of bone or tortoiseshell, and suggest that the very peculiar

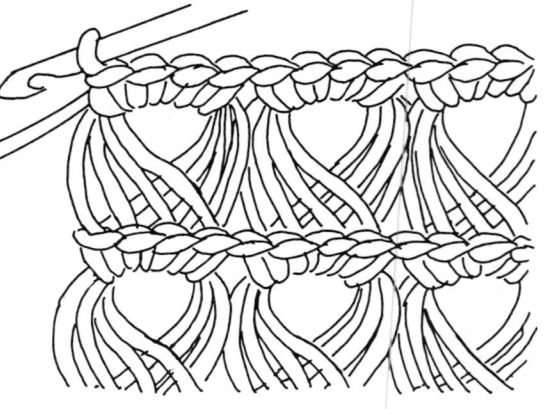

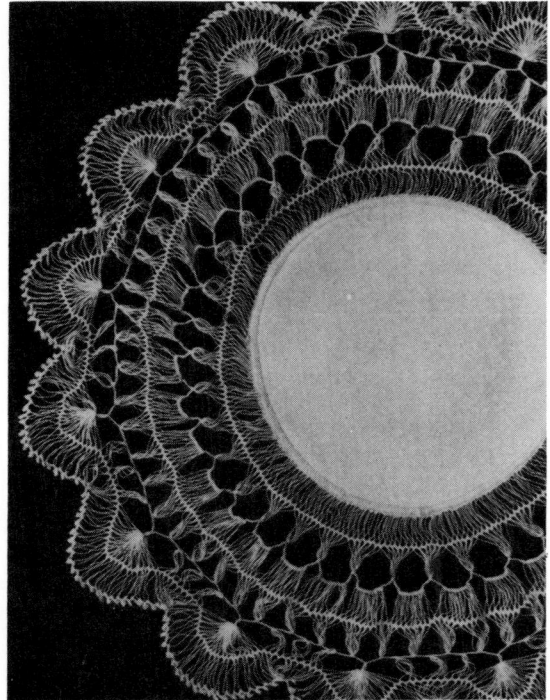

Illust. 37 One of a set of table mats in hairpin crochet.

long hook for holding a row of stitches. It occurred frequently in Victorian publications under the name of *Tricot crochet* or *Tricotee*, from the French term for knitting. It was also called *German crochet* until the advent of the First World War disgraced this name. *Railway crochet, Fool's crochet* or *Idiot crochet* were alternatives. In America it was known as *Afghan crochet*, a reference to its use for travelling rugs called afghans. In France it was known as *Crochet Victoria* and *Crochet Tunisien*.

Tunisian crochet is recognisable by a weave of horizontal threads running through the vertical threads on the front surface of the work. It is

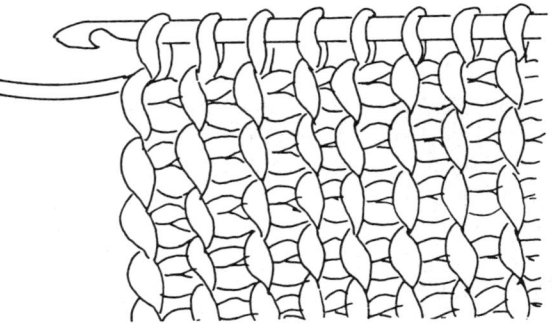

Fig. 8 Tunisian crochet.

that thread is looped around a prong. Each stitch is placed in the preceding loop. A wider centre braid can be formed by working two or more stitches each time instead of the usual single stitch.

Broomstick crochet, known until its recent revival by the more beguiling name of *Peacock's Eye*, is a technique where extra large loops are grouped at regular intervals to form an open 'eye'. A very similar form of knitting is known by the same name, and indeed it is often hard to tell them apart. A gauge of some sort is needed on which to form the loops, and whereas a slip of cardboard or a finger once sufficed, a long needle or 'broomstick' of finger thickness is now the norm.

Tunisian crochet is a truly simple skill – a cross between knitting and crochet yet easier to work than either. Once it was known as *Shepherd's Knitting*, and it is a pity that the name has died out, for it was exactly descriptive of the use of a

worked in rows without turning, keeping the front of the work facing all the time. Rows are worked alternately forward from right to left, and backward from left to right, picking up a hookful of stitches on the forward row, and casting them off on the backward row. The basic form of Tunisian crochet corresponds to normal double crochet, but trebles and any other normal crochet stitch, can be transposed into the Tunisian technique. It is feasible to cross, cluster and layer them in all sorts of compound patterns.

Tunisian crochet has one great advantage over normal crochet, it can be cut and seamed. It does not unravel on cutting but merely runs back to the next uncut stitch where it locks. The following terse directions for a 'Waistcoat in

Tricotee', from *Weldon's Practical Crochet*, 4th Series, 1887, show that cutting was a common practice

Required, 10ozs of black 3-thread fleecy wool or double Berlin, and a long bone tricot needle, No. 8. Commence with a chain of 66 stitches, or as many as required to make the width of one of the front pieces, measuring from a cloth waistcoat. Pick up each stitch in succession and work back in the ordinary manner, and continue in plain tricotee row by row till you have a length of 24 inches. Work the other front similarly. Send to a tailor to be made up.

Russian crochet was a name applied in general to any closely worked and warm double crochet stitch, although Weldon's publications describe Russian crochet as ridged double crochet, i.e., the hook is inserted into the back loop of each stitch. This leaves the unworked front loop as a ridge, and consecutive rows of ridged double crochet acquire an attractive corrugation. A Weldon's pattern of 1886 offers 'Stays for a Child of Three' worked in this manner.

Tapestry crochet or *Jacquard crochet*, as the name suggests, is a close textured multi-coloured technique. It is more natural to work this in continuous rounds, for the reversal of rows can present problems when several colours are handled at once. Four threads can be manipulated at the same time, without dropping them, if two are held on the left hand, and two on the right. In order to achieve an exact division of colour, without bleeding, threads are changed before working the last draw-through which completes a stitch.

Multi-coloured patterns look best in a plain stitch, such as trebles or double crochet, the latter being a favourite since this has a more tapestry-like appearance. Fine tapestry crochet worked in silk was once quite common, and survives in countries of the eastern Mediterranean. Tapestry braids worked in slip stitch, in the same direction throughout, can resemble tablet weaving, and are known as *Bosnian crochet*.[5]

Turkish crochet[6] is noted not only for its silk tapestry designs but for its *oyas*, which are decorative trimmings of extraordinary ingenuity. These often imitate flower and fruit forms, and are finely worked on a small scale in plain double crochet, to resemble the more highly-prized needlepoint *oyas*.

Patchwork crochet is self-explanatory, although there are two types. The patches can be of fabric, edged and pieced together with crochet, or they can be worked entirely in crochet, as in the case of the well-known granny squares, which have appeared so often over the years for charity blankets and similar marathon efforts.

Beaded crochet, formerly worked with silk thread, is a very easy technique. The beads are threaded in reverse order of requirement and slipped up into position at the back of the crochet as work progresses. The back is therefore planned as the right side, and it is best to work continuously in the same direction, in rounds.

Fig. 9 Crochet moulds manufactured by Carl Mez of Germany, circa 1890.

Ring crochet or *Moulded crochet* is another recurrent fad, which began as a rather childish use of brass curtain rings covered with double crochet. It gained popularity as a furnishing crochet in the 1890s when the work developed into a more elaborate form. Not only did designs include rings-within-rings, but the ring shapes become distorted to form ovals, teardrops, hearts, diamonds, spades, clubs and other appealing forms, for any wired shape can be covered with double crochet stitches. This type of crochet was often worked in metallic threads or in pearl cottons of variegated shades.

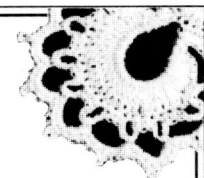

5
MATERIALS AND EQUIPMENT

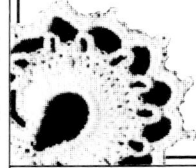

When threads were hand spun they were sold in skeins, and the custom of marketing in this way persisted long after the introduction of mechanical spinning. The size, or count, of a thread was a number which referred originally to the number of skeins per pound weight; the finer the thread the higher the number.

Between the years 1839 and 1852, John Mercer, a textile engineer of Lancashire, was granted a series of patents relating to improvements in the manufacture of thread. He was the original inventor of the mercerisation process, later modified by Horace Lowe, also of Lancashire, in 1889. Mercerisation strengthens the thread and imparts a permanent lustrous finish.

Unprocessed cottons continued to be manufactured after the introduction of mercerised cottons, and in fact many workers preferred them. However the sizing of these threads can present problems to a modern worker who wishes to follow an old pattern. The following table [1] gives a comparison of sizes for non-mercerised and mercerised crochet cottons. Although it refers specifically to Ardern's products, it can be taken as a general guide to most British and American cotton sizes.

There were numerous manufacturers, including Copley Marshall, Dewhursts, Evans, Peri Lusta and Strutts, but the most prolific was undoubtedly Arderns, established in 1856, who sustained a vigorous advertising campaign with an enticing line in sales appeal. Most manufacturers produced a range of different types of cotton, and it can be difficult now to distinguish between the mercerised and non-mercerised in pattern directions, unless the name or number gives a clue. Coat's famed *Mercer Crochet* was first registered in 1885.

Fine crochet cottons were manufactured only in white or in the unbleached and half-bleached shades. Coloured threads *were* available, but they were the thicker and softer types such as pearl cottons and silks, more suited to embroidery. These were two-cord twists, which absorb a dye easily, whereas the fine crochet cottons were tougher six-cord twists. Coats first began to advertise their range of coloured *Mercer Crochet* circa 1930.

When hooks were hand-made, steel hooks were finished with a separate handle, usually of bone or ivory, and this practice continued after the mechanisation of hook making. A patent granted in 1848 to Henry Walker[2], manufacturer

Ardern's Crochet Cotton (non-mercerised)	8	10	14	18	20	22	24	30	36	40	50
Ardern's Sylko Crochet (mercerised)	10	15	20	30	40	50	60	70	80	100	150

The Envy of Your Friends

Beautiful handiwork is a just source of pride — the envy of all who behold it. No work is more gratifying than crochet, especially when made with Ardern's Crochet Cotton.

All Ardern's Cottons — from the finest to the coarsest — have that exquisite finish so much admired. After years of service and frequent washing, lace made with Ardern's still retains its freshness of appearance.

Let your crochet be the envy of your friends —
and to make it, always use

Ardern's
Crochet Cotton

A favourite over sixty years ago, Ardern's is now more popular than ever. It is the 'make' that ladies' papers recommend ; whilst designers and workers of original patterns regularly use it.

Sold in White in all numbers from 00 to 60. In a good range of Colours in No. 8.

Get the Crochet habit — always ask for Ardern's.

Stocked by Drapers and Needlework Dealers everywhere.

Reprint 1 Advertisement in *Fancy Needlework Illustrated*, 1914.

Reprint 2 Advertisement in *Fancy Needlework Illustrated*, 1915. ➤

Will you join the Army of Women Workers who use

ARDERN'S CROCHET COTTONS?

The most noteworthy change that has arisen through the war is the adaptability of women to many kinds of work hitherto done by men.

A New Army — The Army of Women Workers —

has arisen, who find that the weariness of manual and clerical work is appreciably relieved by a change to the restful pastime of "doing a bit of crochet."

You do not have to tire yourself by walking from shop to shop to buy Ardern's Crochet Cotton, as every up-to-date Draper or Art-Needlework Dealer stocks it.

White, in all numbers, 00 to 60.
Colours, in number 8.

The Pride of Achievement

Ardern's
Crochet Cotton

Your tea-cloth — or other crochet work — will be a source of pride to you and a delight to your friends if done with Ardern's Crochet Cotton.

Always pleasant to use because of its smooth and even quality and snowy whiteness. Also you get the satisfying reward of durability in wear — a big consideration, especially nowadays.

Ardern's represents British Manufacture at its best.

Sold by up-to-date Drapers and all the best Art-Needlework Dealers. White, in all numbers—Colours in No. 8.

(Instructions for working this pattern are given in No. 52 of "Fancy Needlework Illustrated.")

This Happy Hour

There's nothing more pleasant than the happy hour or two spent in friendly chatter and restful crocheting.

Ardern's Crochet Cotton doubles the pleasure of this delightful occupation, because it is such a smooth-finished easy thread to work with, and produces such lovely lacy effects. Moreover its snowy-whiteness, and durability can be thoroughly depended on in wash and wear. It has stood the test for over 60 years.

Ardern's
CROCHET COTTON

Drapers and Art-Needlework Dealers everywhere stock Ardern's Crochet Cotton —White in all numbers. Colours in No. 8 only.

N.B. If requiring Mercerised Crochet, use Ardern's "Sylko" Crochet White in Nos. 10 to 150.

◄ Reprint 3 Advertisement in *Fancy Needlework Illustrated*, 1922. The Tea-Set design in filet crochet first appeared in *Fancy Needlework Illustrated* in 1913.

Reprint 4 Advertisement in *Leach's Home Needlework Series*, 1928.

Reprint 5 Advertisement in *Weldon's 300 Crochet Ideas*, 1920s.

The Favourite Cotton for Lovely Crochet

Many women can show with pride to-day beautiful crochet lace made long years ago with Ardern's Crochet Cotton. Use it yourself and you will feel the same pleasure and satisfaction.

There are four things which keep Ardern's a prime favourite — snowy whiteness, smooth and even texture, exquisite finish, and superior washing qualities.

Ardern's Crochet Cotton

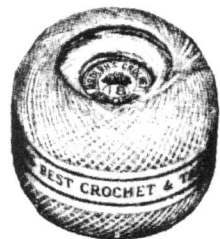

Made in Britain by British labour for over 60 years.

Ensure the success of your crochet, and the fullest satisfaction to yourself, by asking for Ardern's Crochet Cotton at any good Drapers or Art-Needlework Dealers. White in all numbers, and colours in No. 8.

of the *Penelope* hook, refers to 'certain improvements in the manufacture of a particular description of needles, known in the trade as crôchet tambour, and sometimes as hook needles and crôchet hooks'. His invention concerned the striking of dies to cut a pair of hooks simultaneously, head to head.

Chamber's Perfected Crochet and Tambour Holders and Needles, very similar to the *Penelope* hook, were advertised in Mlle Riego's *Crochet Book*, 5th Series, 1849, with the assertion, 'Ladies requiring a perfect and complete set of Crochet or Tambour Holders and Needles are recommended to use the above articles which have been tested and manufactured under the direction of Mdlle Riego de la Branchardière'.

Accidents were not uncommon with fine steel hooks, *The Young Ladies' Journal: Complete Guide to the Worktable*, in 1884, felt obliged to issue a warning: 'We take the opportunity of cautioning

ladies . . . that it is scarcely possible to remove a steel hook from the flesh without the aid of a surgeon'.

Collectable hooks can still be found which once belonged to matching sets of workbox tools. The mother-of-pearl hook shown was once part of such a set. It has a hand-made steel hook with a silver collar.

Accurate sizing became feasible with manufactured hooks, although it was not always considered important. Many a late-Victorian pattern began, 'Procure a rather fine steel crochet

Fig. 10 Key to Illust. 38.
A, a bone Tunisian hook; B, mid-nineteenth century bone hook; C, the Penelope *hook; D, mid-nineteenth century hook with removable handle; E, mother-of-pearl handle with a silver collar; F, late-nineteenth century hooks; G, early-twentieth century hooks (the* Eclipse *is the hook with a flattened shank); H, early-twentieth century steel hairpin fork.*

Illust. 38 For identification see Fig. 10.

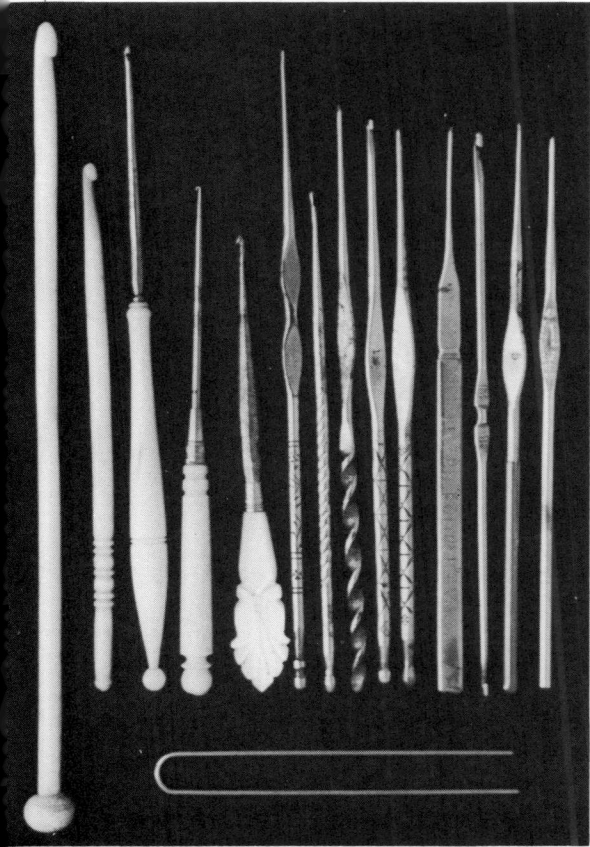

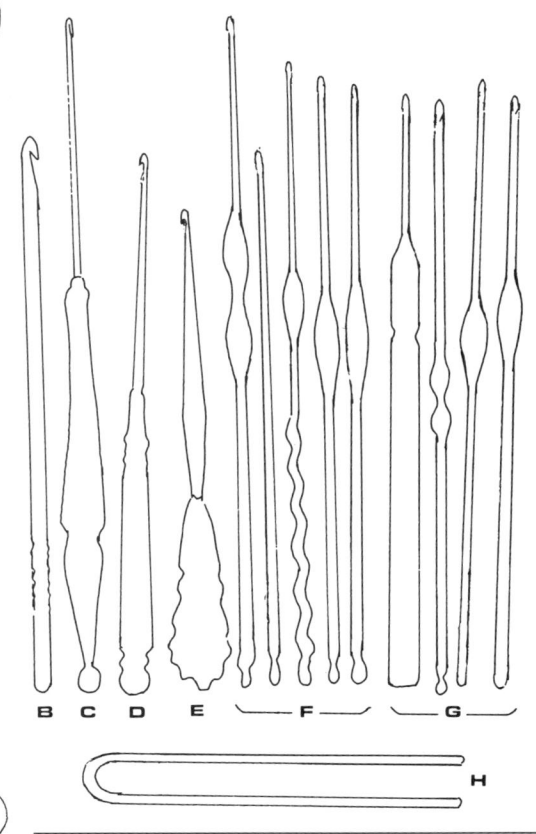

needle', relying on the worker to match hook to thread herself (which is still the best method). Henry Walker, manufacturer of the *Penelope* hook, introduced the *Bell* gauge (in bell form) which was a duo knitting needle and crochet hook gauge. It seems to have been the first to enable an accurate measurement of size.

Steel hooks were frequently nickel plated, and they gradually became more streamlined until they assumed their present form in the Edwardian era. However, there was a great deal of experimentation to find an optimum functional form, judging by the number of

Fig. 11 Steel hook with a fan-shaped extension as a thumb rest, patented in 1896.

Fig. 12 Steel hook with an ingenious thumb rest, patented in 1903.

abandoned patent claims. Some were telescopic and some had multiple folding hooks which closed like a penknife. Morris and Yeoman's *Kaurkuk*, advertised in 1912, had a removable cork handle, Shrimpton's *Eclipse*, advertised in 1914, had an unusual flattened shank, and Milward's *Super Archer* had a gold-plated head.

The very practical Edwardian hooks were numbered differently from the Victorian *Bell* range. A comparison of old steel hook sizes with their modern counterparts is given in the following table. It should be taken as a guide only for the metric sizes do not correspond exactly.

Large 'wool' hooks have always been gauged in the same range as knitting needles. Old specimens can be found in boxwood, bone, tortoiseshell, vulcanite, etc. Any hook with a knob on the end is intended for Tunisian crochet, and some large Tunisian hooks screwed together in three parts, rather like a chimney sweep's brush. These were intended for making blankets.

There were various arrangements for keeping a ball of thread clean and free-running during work, although an adequate homely receptacle was a jam jar on the floor. The popular bracelet devices, such as the *Terry* and the *Wristlet* crochet ball holders, were available in rolled gold, solid silver, silver plate and nickel plate. The holder shown is the *Wristlet*, patented in 1912[3]. These holders could be removed from the bracelet and pinned to the waist or bosom, or hung on a special free-standing table stand.

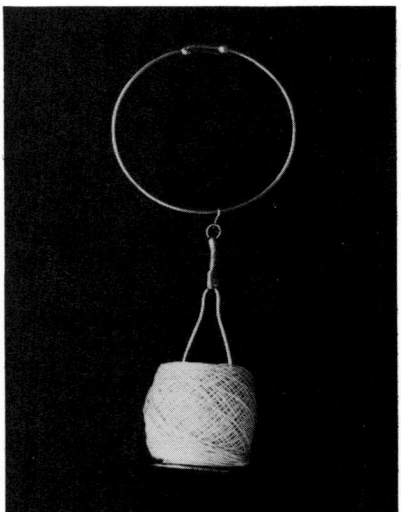

Illust. 39 A crochet ball holder.

Bell sizes	14		16		18		20		22		24		26		
Edwardian sizes	1	1½	2	2½	3	3½	4	4½	5	5½	6	6½	7	7½	8
New metric sizes	2.00		1.75	1.50	1.25		1.00		0.75		0.60				

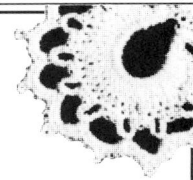

6
PRESERVATION
AND STORAGE

The value of a specimen of old crochet can only be assessed by its owner, for family or personal associations may have to be taken into consideration, apart from any intrinsic worth following from excellence of workmanship and design, or from age.

Illust. 41 There were many variations on this wheel theme. A prototype appeared in Needlecraft, No. 41, 1908.

Full honour should always be accorded to Irish crochet of a standard comparable to the best shown in chapter 3, for such work is precious and should be conserved with reverence. In fact any crochet sufficiently worthy in character, or of unusual historic or geographic interest, should

Illust. 40 A lacey doyley design, well worth studying for its method of increasing.

Illust. 42 A plain filet crochet edging, worked in straight lengths without a mitred corner.

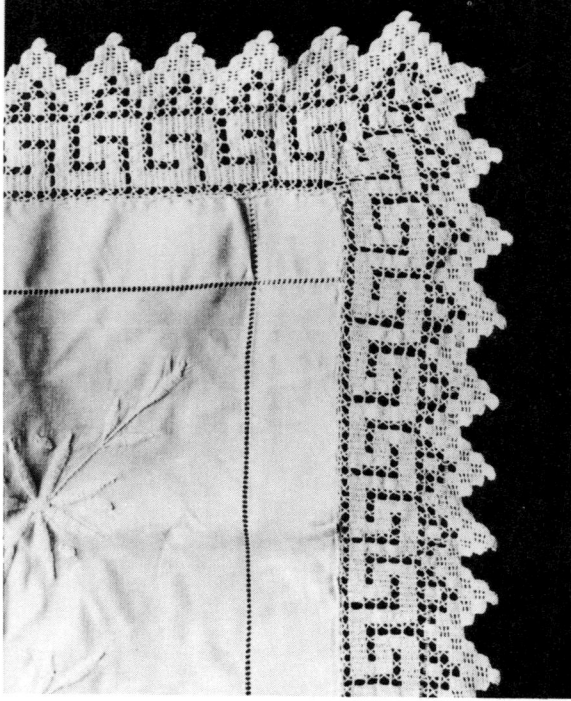

Illust. 43 Filet guipure crochet in a Greek key design. The pattern was given in Weldon's Practical Needlework, *circa 1895.*

Illust. 44 A heavy window-blind edging, circa 1918.

be treasured. Many old doyleys are so ingenious in theme and so rich in detail, that they should be kept as a record of pattern sophistry.

However, there is an abundance of filet crochet of rather simple accomplishment, such as the cloths shown in Illusts 42 and 43, and since there is a good deal of it around, it is hardly worth preserving for its own sake. Similarly, much of the humble torchon crochet scarcely qualifies as important. One may as well use and enjoy these,

Illust. 45 Edging from a sheet-sham. A sheet-sham was a ➤ *partial top-sheet with a decorated turn-back, more easily washed than an entire sheet.*

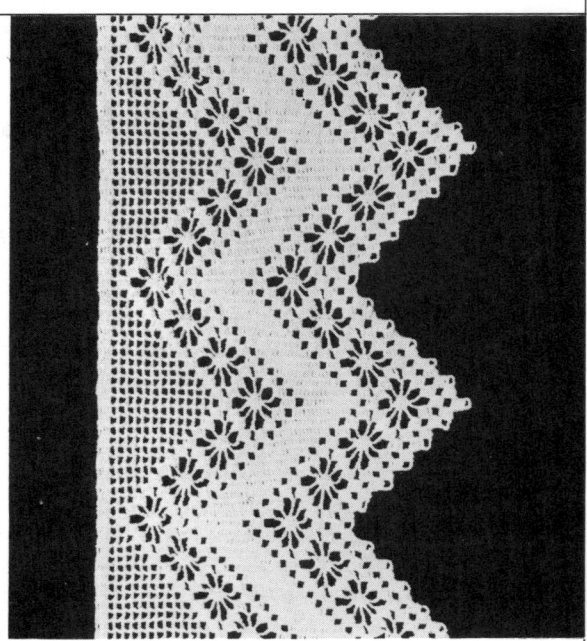

together with one's best china and memories of a more gracious way of life.

Normal household washing is drastic treatment for any aged textile. Cotton crochet can be washed repeatedly with pure soap without harm, but additives such as the optical whiteners and bleaching compounds of present-day washing agents can be potentially destructive. Only the very mildest products should be used[1] in soft warm water. A final rinse in distilled, or boiled and cooled water, will ensure the purest possible finish.

It is important that crochet does not dry in a dishevelled state, so while it is still wet, pat it out flat on a clean absorbent cloth. All crochet contracts with washing and will benefit from being blocked into shape. To do this, stretch the work well, although not excessively, so that the pattern is accurately displayed, and pin all around the circumference with stainless steel or brass pins. Small pieces can be pinned on an ironing board, larger items on a cloth spread on the floor carpet. Leave all pins in place until the work is quite dry, and then ironing should be unnecessary. Most of the specimens shown in this book were blocked thus in preparation for photography, and this is the reason why they look so fresh and pristine despite their age.

However, it is not always feasible to pin out a large amount of crochet which is attached to linen, for the fabric itself will require ironing. In this case, press while still slightly damp, under an ironing cloth, at the lowest setting manageable, for excessive heat can be damaging to old fibres.

The average household airing cupboard is quite the wrong place for permanent storage of old crochet or indeed of any other textile. Excessive dryness is to be avoided, as should over-exposure to sunlight or ultra-violet light, exposure to dust, sulphur fumes and general atmospheric pollution, or a damp atmosphere.

Illust. 46 A heavy and very large edging, probably intended for a bedspread.

HERITAGE CROCHET: AN ANALYSIS

Cotton is not itself vulnerable to attack by moth grubs or beetles, but adhering starch can provide a source of food. Crochet which is to be stored for any length of time should therefore be put away in a starch-free state. Mildews, also, can be troublesome on cotton which has been starched.

As Karen Finch and Greta Putnam point out, in their book, *Caring for Textiles*[2], the ideal storage place is a tomb – cool, dry and dark, of constant temperature and humidity, unpolluted and undisturbed – although they do not actually say, 'Take it with you'.

Crochet should be stored flat, well protected with acid-free tissue paper. Any work too large for flat storage is best rolled on a cardboard cylinder, but this too should be wrapped with tissue before the work is rolled. If folding is unavoidable, more tissue should be used to pad the folds and avoid a sharp crease.

Any scraps unworthy of preservation in themselves may still be worth keeping as material for the repair of better specimens. Non-mercerised crochet cottons are virtually unobtainable now, and can only be gleaned from old work. When unpicking thread for this purpose, wind it on a wire frame, such as a cake cooler, and rinse in warm water to straighten it. Usually, crochet which has been made from motifs is easy to repair, as a complete motif can be replaced, but crochet worked in rows can be a greater problem, for if the damage extends over several rows then a great deal may need to be replaced. A slight tear may reasonably be disguised by sewing, but if possible repairs should be effected with a hook rather than with a needle. Use the finest hook manageable for the task, but if a hook continually splits the thread then it is too fine. If on completion a difference in tension is apparent, it can usually be corrected by damping and easing the new repair.

It may be more expedient not to repair an old and precious specimen, but to tack it to a fabric backing so that its weaknesses are supported. For this purpose, choose a dark fabric (for white crochet) without a pronounced weave, and it should be an old or washed fabric, devoid of harmful dressing. A well-chosen frame will invest mounted work with an extra quality of esteem.

In preparation for framing, lay the fabric over a board and lace it tautly across the back. The montage can then be framed in the usual manner as a picture, although any glass should rest on a surrounding mat in order to avoid pressure on the crochet. It would seem appropriate to choose a frame of the same age as the lace, but in practice old frames tend to be too heavy in appearance and a lighter modern frame is often better.

Illust. 47 Assorted samples, circa 1910 to 1920.

Old sample books should be inspected for pins, as these will invariably have rusted, and the offenders should be removed and replaced with

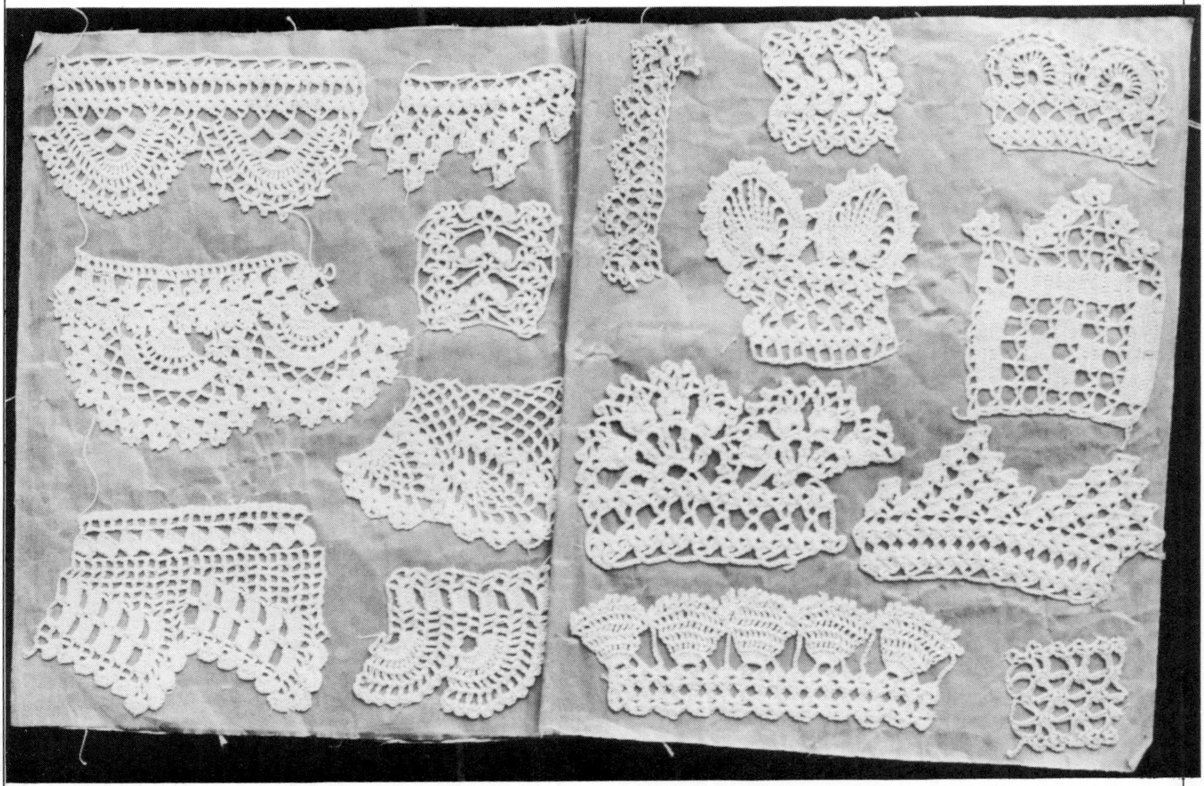

Illust. 48 A sample book of pink-coloured glazed calico, circa 1910.

tacking cotton. However, it is better to accept the rust marks than attempt to remove them and further weaken the fibres. On the whole it is advisable to leave the samples in position, rather than remove them for cleaning, and so perhaps destroy the book's validity as a historic record. Samples mounted on glazed calico can safely be damped with distilled water and gently stretched out to their original shape, as they will have contracted with age. Do only one page of samples at a time to allow each to dry out properly, and of course this treatment is only suitable for pages which are waterproof.

Illust. 49 Another page of samples, circa 1910. ➤

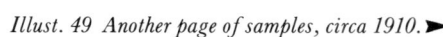

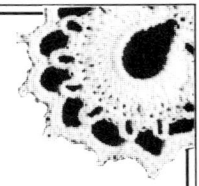

7

PUBLISHED SOURCES
OF INFORMATION

The earliest printed patterns were published by retail establishments for needlework requisites as an aid to sales. Small in format – 16° or 24° – with hand-coloured engravings, gilt edges and a delectable style of prose, they discreetly proclaimed the vendor's wares and even offered tuition. A stream of such publications appeared in the 1840s, with patterns ranging from the comely to the ridiculous, and no doubt including those which caused George Eliot's caustic comment. Pattern ephemera such as single-folded sheets or broadsides, were common in the

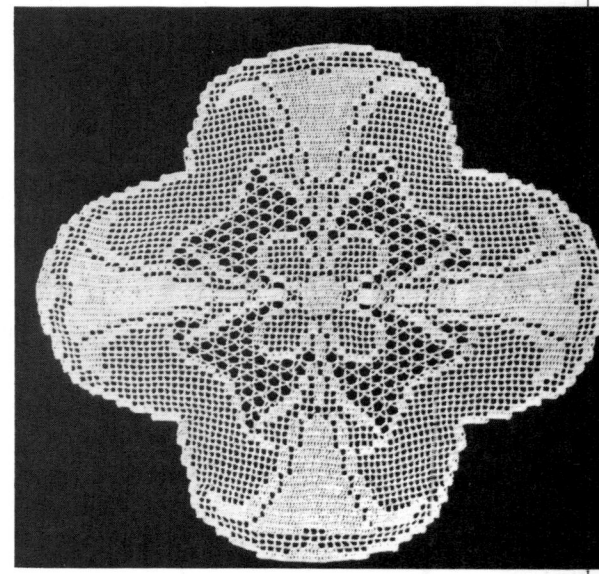

Illust. 50 This magnificent tulip edging, ten inches wide, was designed by Mrs Hodgett for Leach's Tea Time Crochet *(Leach's Home Needlework, Nos 2 and 7) in 1915. Mrs Hodgett designed almost exclusively for Leach's.*

Illust. 51 A lily design, also by Mrs Hodgett, for Leach's Home Needlework, *Nos 54 and 65, reprinted in No. 127 in 1928. The piece shown is intended as the centre inset of a tea cloth, with a matching border 11 inches deep.*

1850s; penny patterns of this type were on sale at the Great Exhibition at the Crystal Palace in 1851.

Among the first pioneers were Mrs Jane Gaugain of Edinburgh, who published *The Lady's Assistant for executing useful and fancy designs in Knitting, Netting and Crochetwork* in 1840, and Miss Frances Lambert of London, who produced *The*

Handbook of Needlework in 1842. In close pursuit were Mr and Mrs George Curling Hope of Ramsgate and Mrs Cornelia Mee of Bath, with an assortment of booklets dating from 1842, Mrs Eliza Warren of Holloway, who offered *The Point-Lace Crochet Collar Book* in 1846, and Mlle Eléonore Riego of London, who began a prolific publishing career with *Knitting, Crochet and Netting* in 1846.

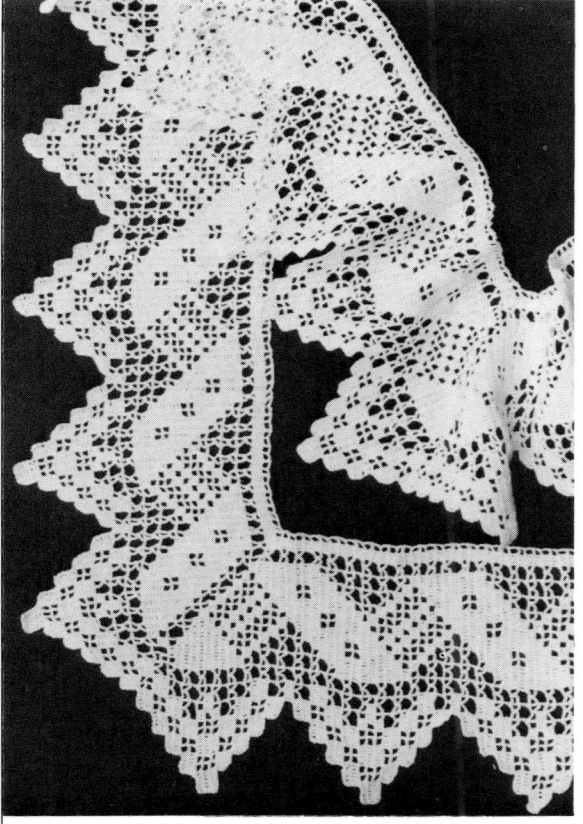

Illust. 52 This attractive ribbon design was given in Weldon's Practical Needlework, *No. 321, 1912.*

There was a plethora of following publications, and many other authors, too numerous to mention individually, but an excellent comprehensive account is given by Esther Potter in *English Knitting and Crochet Books of the Nineteenth Century* (*see* Bibliography).

Piracy of designs seems to have been a problem right from the beginning, for Miss Lambert, in her later editions of *The Handbook of Needlework*, refers to 'numerous petty piracies . . . in America . . . which she is fain to accept as a compliment'.

Mlle Eléonore Riego de la Branchardière, who published her works simply as Mlle (or Mdlle) Riego, is an important figure in the world of crochet. Born in England of an Irish mother and a French father in exile after the Revolution, she was a wondrous creative needlewoman, designer and 'teacher at court', justly proud of having won the only gold medal for crochet at the Great Exhibition – with an angelic child's dress of the very finest lace. She went on to produce a monthly journal called *The Needle*, and claimed to have written in all over 100 books on needlework. With her Irish connections, Mlle Riego had been instrumental in helping to raise the standards of crochet and other laces in Ireland, and for this reason, on her death, she left a substantial part of her fortune as a trust fund, with the aim of improving the lot of needy women engaged in these tasks in Ireland.

A posthumous selection of her patterns, *The Selected Works of Mdlle Riego*, edited by Mrs Rivers-Turnbull, was published in four volumes from 1904. Mlle Riego's original publications are now collector's items and are much sought after. The following list of her titles on crochet has been compiled from the British Museum Library catalogue, although it does not necessarily represent her full output on the subject:

Knitting, Crochet and Netting	1846
The Crochet Book, 1st Series to 18th Series	1847 to 1856
The Crochet Winter Book	1848
The Bead Crochet Book	1855
The Crochet Winter Book for 1857	1857
Gold Stars in Tatting and Crochet	1861
Waved Crochet Braid Antimacassars and Doyleys	1861
Waved Crochet Braid Collars	1861
Waved Crochet Braid Trimmings	1861
The Second Book of Waved Braid Trimmings	1862

Following from the gradual repeals of various taxes relating to the paper trade in the 1850s to 60s, and from the introduction of wood pulp for newsprint in the 1870s, several women's papers and magazines, such as *The Queen, The Young Ladies' Journal* and *The Ladies' Treasury*, flourished in the latter half of the nineteenth century. These all included a regular feature on needlework which proved so popular that it paved the way for a series of journals wholly devoted to this need, which were launched in the 1880s. They were of 4° format and delightfully packed with patterns and practical information. The engravings alone, with their painstaking attention to detail, must have kept large armies of illustrators in employment.

The most important publisher was undoubtedly Weldon, whose productions included the journal *Weldon's Practical Needlework*. As Weldon ran an efficient subscription service both at home and overseas, it is not unusual to find 'colonial editions' still in unexpected corners of the erstwhile Empire. *Weldon's Practical Needlework* ran from 1886 (Vol. 1) to 1930 (Vol. 45). There were 12 issues per year, undated, but it is easy to calculate publication dates, for instance, Vol. 17, No. 204 was published in December 1902. Each issue featured a particular subject, and over 200 of these were sub-titled *Weldon's Practical Crochet*. The most popular were repeatedly re-printed.

Weldon ultimately developed a splendid range of journals. *Weldon's Practical Needlework – New Series*, re-numbered after 1930, reached No. 404 by 1959. *Weldon's Sixpeny Series*, which ran

Reprint 6 Cover of *Weldon's Practical Needlework*, No. ➤ 42, published in 1889.

from 1921 (No. 1) to 1936 (No. 341), and contained a number of issues devoted to crochet, dropped its monetary epithet to continue as *Weldon's Series* from 1936 (No. 342) to 1939 (No. 479), when it progressed to *Weldon's Fashion Series*. However, the crochet content of these gradually diminished over the years. There were several less frequent runs; *Weldon's New Crochet Series* was a bi-monthly, and *Weldon's Beautiful Needlework* a quarterly.

Another prolific range was that of Leach's, which began with *Mrs. Leach's Practical Fancy Work Basket* in 1886. Mrs Clara Leach's monthly journal contained a plentiful amount of crochet, and had reached Vol. 22 by 1906. There were several other publications, such as *Leach's Penny Crochet*, which began in the late 1890s and ran until 1909, to continue as *Leach's Ladies Work and Crochet* (and *Leach's Ladies Work: Crochet*) from 1909 to 1912, and which reverted again to *Leach's Penny Crochet* in 1913. Inflation in the 1920s necessitated a change of title to *Leach's Sixpenny Series*, which allocated special issues to crochet. *Leach's Home Needlework* ran to 144 issues, from 1915 to 1930.

Major hard-cover books from the late nineteenth century include *Weldon's Practical Shilling Guide to Fancy Work*, which was first published in the 1870s and ran to 14 editions, changing its appellation to *Weldon's Practical Guide to Fancy Work* in 1922. It underwent a complete metamorphosis to emerge finally as the *Weldon's Needlework Encyclopaedia* in 1924. *Beeton's Book of Needlework* was first published in 1870, and the *Dictionary of Needlework* by S.F.A. Caulfeild and B.C. Saward first appeared in 1882. *The Young Ladies' Journal: Complete Guide to the Worktable* saw its first edition in 1884, and Thérèse de Dillmont's famous *Encyclopedia of Needlework* was first published in France in 1886. The latter was subsequently translated into English, German, Italian and Spanish, which is no doubt why such a vast following of women still look on it as their 'bible'.

No. 42, Vol. 4. WELDON'S PRACTICAL NEEDLEWORK. Price 2d. Monthly.

WELDON'S PRACTICAL CROCHET.

PRICE 2D

EIGHTH SERIES.
31 ILLUSTRATIONS. COMPLETE.

How to Crochet Gloves, Boots, Shawls, Dresses, Petticoats, Muff, Boa, &c.

Baby's Boot in Fancy Tricot.

Low-Neck Dress.

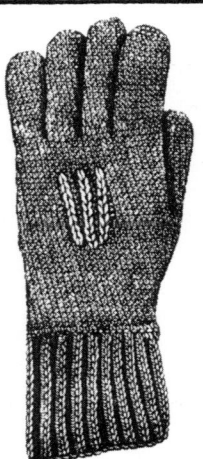

Gentleman's Glove.

Baby's Rattle.

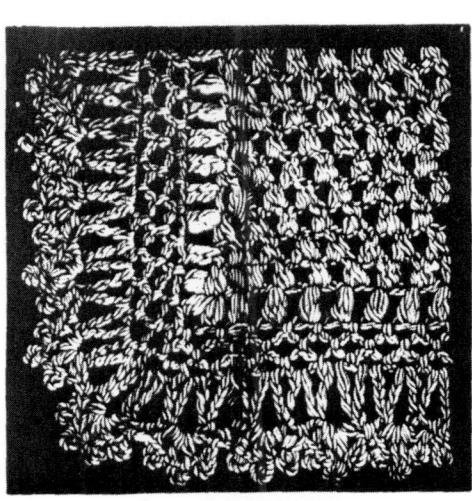

Shawl in Cane Pattern.

Child's Boa.

CONTENTS.

EIGHTH SERIES.

WELDON & CO., Publishers, 7, Southampton Street, Strand, London, W.C.

WELDON'S

Always in Print.

PRACTICAL

Seventy-Seventh Series.

PRICE
2D..
COMPLETE.

CROCHET

EDGINGS.

9 Illustrations.

How to Crochet Useful Laces, with Corners for same, suited to all Purposes.

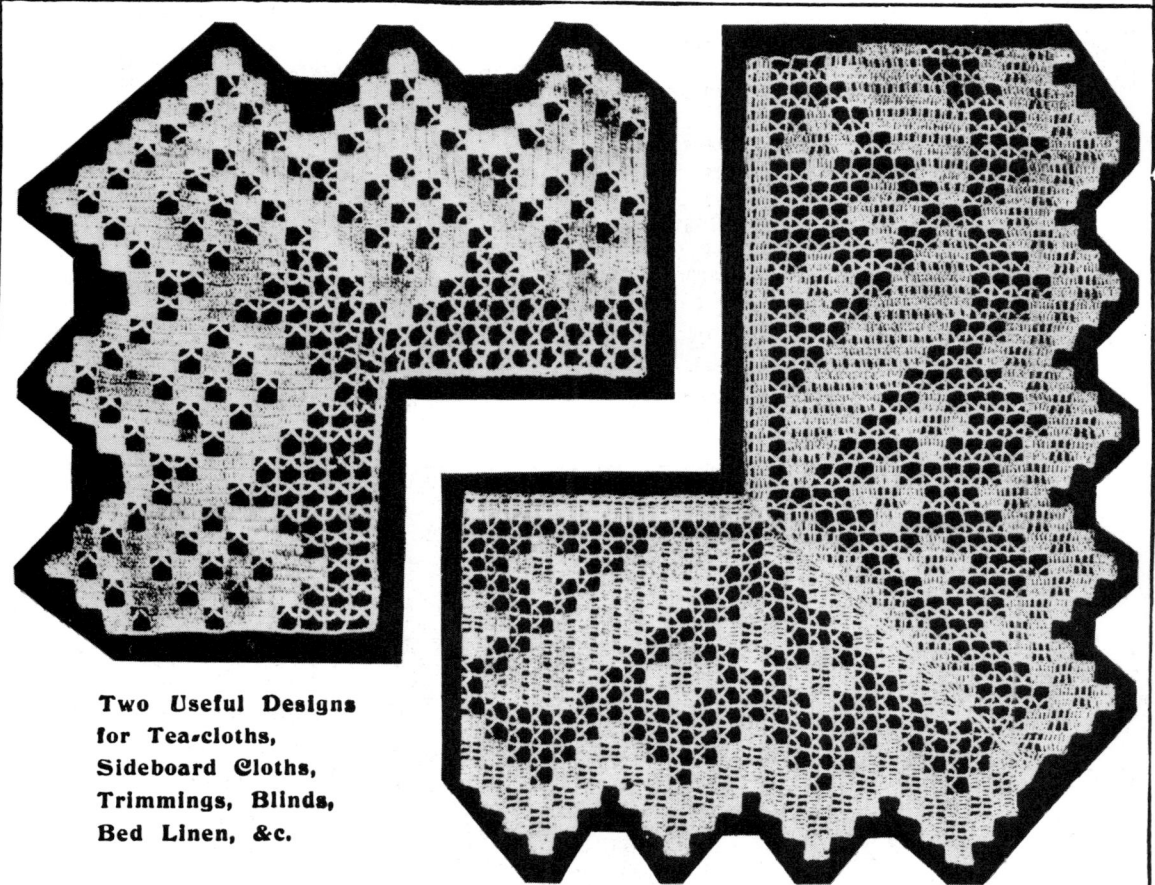

Two Useful Designs
for Tea-cloths,
Sideboard Cloths,
Trimmings, Blinds,
Bed Linen, &c.

◄ Reprint 7 Cover of *Weldon's Practical Needlework*, No. 230, published in 1905.

Reprint 8 Cover of *Needlecraft*, No. 27, published in 1906.

Needlecraft
Practical Journal.

Price **2**D.

Irish Crochet Lace.

WITH 26 PHOTO-ILLUSTRATIONS DIRECT FROM THE ORIGINAL WORK.

Fig. 23—A Dessert D'Oyley, or Pincushion Top, in Irish Crochet Lace.

For Description of Working, see page 13.

Needlecraft

A Practical Journal Descriptive and Illustrative of

Price 2 D.

Crochet D'Oyleys

17 PHOTOGRAPHIC ILLUSTRATIONS OF NEW & ORIGINAL D'OYLEY PATTERNS.

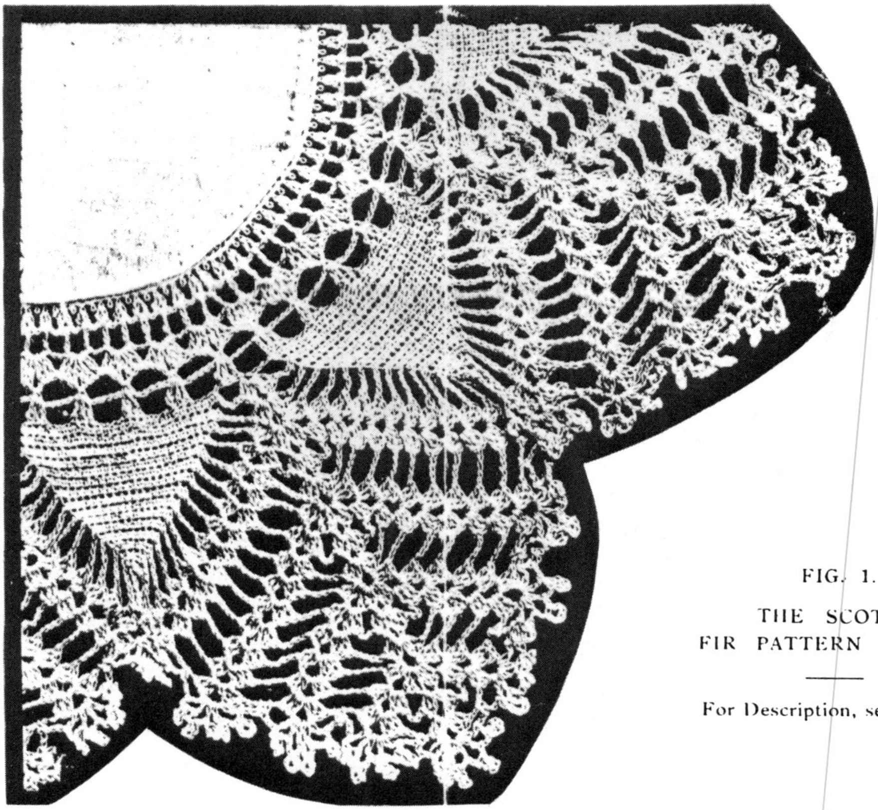

FIG. 1.

THE SCOTCH
FIR PATTERN D'OYLEY.

For Description, see page 3.

Published by THE MANCHESTER SCHOOL OF EMBROIDERY,
MANCHESTER.
(REGISTERED).

No. 26—Vol. 3.]   PUBLISHED QUARTERLY.   PRICE ONE PENNY.
Postage 1d. extra.

A
POPULAR
NUMBER

285,000 Copies printed

CHOICE
CROCHET
PATTERNS

No.-2602.
Section of
"BERYL" LACE.

No.- 2603. "DRESDEN" CROCHET LACE, WITH CORNER AND TRIANGLE.

◄Reprint 9 Cover of *Needlecraft*, No. 41, published in 1908.

Reprint 10 Cover of *Fancy Needlework Illustrated*, No. 26, published in 1913.

Towards the end of the nineteenth century, wholesale manufacturers (as opposed to the former retailers) entered the field of pattern publishing. Thérèse de Dillmont's book was produced by Dollfus-Mieg et Cie, (D.M.C.), thread manufacturers of Mulhouse in Alsace. Similarly, the spinners John Paton Son and Co. Ltd, of Alloa in Scotland, produced *Knitting and Crocheting Book*, compiled by M. Elliot Scrivenor, in 1896.

When the photogravure process for printing became common at the turn of the century, a distinct improvement in quality was noticeable. Flora Klickmann, known for her *Flower Patch* novels and for her extensive editorial work on the *Girl's Own Paper*, edited a range of charming hard-cover books on needlework called *The Home Art Series*. This covetable series includes the following:

The Craft of the Crochet Hook	1912
The Home Art Crochet Book	1912
The Modern Crochet Book	1913
Artistic Crochet	1914
Beautiful Crochet on Household Linen	1916
Distinctive Crochet	1919

Two luxury journals important for their crochet content were *Fancy Needlework Illustrated*, a quarterly published by the Northern School of Art Needlework in Manchester, which ran from 1907 to 1939, and *Needlecraft Practical Journal*.

Needlecraft Practical Journal and *Needlecraft* were one and the same series, with a fugitive sub-title. It began in 1903, with an average of seven issues per year, and ran until the outbreak of war in 1939. Individual issues were devoted to different subjects. Confusingly, its publishers also produced *Needlecraft Monthly Magazine*, of a more general content, also known as *Needlecraft*. This began in 1907.

There was the *Lady's World Fancy Work Book*, a quarterly, which ran from 1906 into the 1920s, and the *Bestway* series of publications, prominent in the 1930s. *Stitchcraft* entered the arena in 1932. The 1930s to 40s were distinguished by the dizzy numbers of manufacturer's leaflets, and by the popular books of J. & P. Coats Ltd, and of Wm Briggs & Co. Ltd, the latter with their *Penelope* range.

Patons & Baldwins' *Woolcraft*, from which so many women learnt to crochet, was first published by J. & J. Baldwin circa 1916, and continued for many years after the two companies merged in 1920.

Alas, the identity of an individual designer was seldom known unless she was able to publish her own works – a practice which seems to have been more usual in America. Mary Card was renowned in the 1920s for her ravishing table-cloths in filet crochet, presented in chart form. Anne Orr of Nashville, Tennessee, produced a voluptuous range of needlework designs from the years 1910 to 1945. She was a gifted needlewoman and designer, well-known as needlework editor for *Good Housekeeping*. A fuller account of her work is given in *Crochet Designs of Anne Orr* (*see* Bibliography).

The Priscilla Publishing Co. of Boston issued a wide range of pattern publications, now keenly sought after, as are those of the American Thread Co. of New York, and the Spool Cotton Co., also of New York. Favourites include the *Lily* and *Star* books. Many designs, especially those of J. & P. Coats, crossed the Atlantic, and were common to both English and American collections.

Some were re-printed again and again. Weldon in particular, re-issued many of their earlier lace crochet patterns, for these do not 'date', and it is quite usual to find patterns from the 1880s and 90s appearing in journals of the 1920s and 30s. For instance, the motif shown in Illust. 73, given in *Weldon's Practical Needlework* in 1891, appeared in *Fancy Needlework Illustrated* in 1907, in Anne Orr's *Crochet Designs* in 1935, and again in a Coats' leaflet of the 1950s. Moreover, it has disseminated with only slight variation into numerous other publications. It would be interesting to speculate on Weldon's original source, for the motif relates to a form common in Irish guipure, where the foundation chains were replaced by a cord.

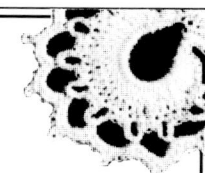

8

STYLES OF
PATTERN WRITING

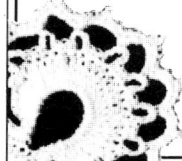

Instructions in many old patterns leave much to be guessed at, and the less lucid leave a suspicion that they may be some primitive form of intelligence test. In the absence of a standard style, written instructions depended on the individual writer's clarity of perception, which naturally varied a good deal.

Much filet crochet entailed not only marathon efforts with hook and thread, but also marathon efforts of pattern writing, for instructions were usually given in full, and it was easy to lose one's way in the maze of print. Workers were sometimes advised to stick a pin in the relevant place. Filet crochet charts, resembling cross-stitch embroidery charts, were customary in American publications. However, they do not seem to have been in general use in England, where written instructions were preferred, and continued until well into the 1930s.

A system of symbols, similar to those used in Part 2 of this book, began to evolve early in the present century, but it proved unpopular and has only reappeared of late years. It is now the usual method of 'writing' in many European and Japanese publications.

The table on page 56 compares some old terms with present day terms for the basic crochet stitches. 'Long treble' or 'long stitch' can be ambiguous, as it may refer to a double treble or triple treble (or to an even longer treble). The difference in present day English and American expressions should be noted.

The examples which follow are original old

patterns, from various sources. Properly, the inner edge of any lace, which is attached to the fabric, is called the foot or footing, and the outer edge is called the head or heading. Old crochet patterns sometimes became confused in their anatomy.

SMALL DOYLEY

Extract from *New Crochet D'oyley Book*, by A Young Lady, 1850. The terse instructions are reasonably clear. The long stitch can be interpreted as double treble.

Use Evan's Boar's Head Crochet Thread No. 26.

First Row: Make a loop, put 28 long stitches into the loop, no chain stitch between.

Second Row: 2 long, 3 chain, 2 long in same loop, 6 chain; repeat 6 times more.

Third Row: D.C. in 3 chain, 6 chain, D.C. in 6 chain; repeat.

Fourth Row: 2 long in 6 chain, 7 chain; repeat.

Fifth Row: 3 D.C. in 7 chain, 9 chain; repeat.

Sixth Row: 10 long, the first 2 to come upon the chain before the first of the 6 long, the last two of the 10 to come upon the 1 chain beyond the 6 long, 3 chain; repeat.

Seventh Row: 8 long, the first to come upon the second long of the 10, 4 chain; repeat.

Eighth Row: 6 long, the same as last row, 6 chain; repeat.

Ninth Row: 4 long, the same as last, 9 chain.

Tenth Row: 2 long above the 4 long, 6 chain, 2

long in centre of the 9 chain; repeat.
Eleventh Row: 2 long above 2 long in 9 chain, 1
chain between them, 8 chain; repeat.
Twelfth Row: 1 round of D.C.

The Border consists of Five Rows.
First Row: 2 long, 5 chain, 2 long, 3 chain,
miss 6 chain on the work, each 2 long in
separate loops, with no chain between.
Second Row: 2 long in 5 chain, 5 chain, 2 long
in same 5 chain, 4 chain, 1 D.C. in centre of

Illust. 53 The Small Doyley. ➤

chain, 4 chain; repeat.
Third Row: 3 long, 5 chain, 3 long in same
loop, 4 chain, 1 D.C. in first 4 chain in last
row, 1 D.C. in second 4 chain, 4 chain; repeat.
Fourth and Fifth Rows: are finished in the same
manner as the Third.

English Present-day	*English Old Forms*	*American Present-day*	*American Old Forms*
chain	chain	chain	chain
slipstitch	single crochet tambour stitch chain stitch	slip stitch	slip stitch single crochet close chain stitch
double crochet	double crochet double tambour plain stitch short stitch	single crochet	single crochet double crochet
half treble	long double crochet short treble	half double crochet	half treble short treble
treble	treble long stitch	double crochet	treble
double treble	long treble long stitch double long stitch	treble	double treble long treble
triple treble	long treble long stitch treble long stitch	double treble	triple treble long treble

then place another short stitch into the upper twin loop at the fourth little loop from joining, chain 3, and 3 long stitches, 3 chain, and 3 long stitches into next loop but one, short stitch into next lower twin loop in the second little loop from joining, and continue round the row. For the last row into each hole between the long stitches put 1 short stitch, 6 chain, 1 short stitch, 9 chain, 1 short stitch, 6 chain and 1 short stitch, then chain 9 and short stitch into the short stitch between the points, 9 more chain, and continue throughout the row.

TWIN LOOP DOYLEY

Extract from *Needlecraft*, No. 41, 1908. For short stitch work double crochet, and refer to the illustration for assistance in solving the puzzle of the loops.

Chain 25, join in a loop, chain 4, work 45 trebles in loop, slip into first, 6 chain and 1 short stitch in every other treble, fasten off neatly. Repeat loop, threading the 25 chain through first loop and then joining into a second loop, and make sufficient of these double loops to form d'oyley. These double loops should be joined to each other by two of the little outside loops of the bottom big loops, to two of the little loops of the top big loop of the next big loop. Sixteen of these twin loops will be found a convenient number for a d'oyley, but this may be varied according to taste. When these are joined into a ring, start the edge at the bottom. On the second loop from the joining, 1 short stitch; 3 chain, 3 long stitches into next but one loop, 3 chain and 3 long stitches into same loop, 3 chain, short stitch into next loop but one, repeat twice;

Illust. 54 The Twin Loop Doyley.

For the Heading:
Put 3 trebles, 3 chain, and 3 trebles into fourth loop from the joining, 3 chain, short stitch into

next loop but one, 3 chain, repeat; then 3 chain and continue the row. For the *2nd Row:* 3 trebles, 3 chain, and 3 trebles into point, then chain 6 and short stitch into short stitch of last row, 6 chain, repeat point, and then without any chain, go on with next point into the next hole, and continue throughout the row. The *3rd Row* is a repetition of the second, only with 9 chain instead of 6. The *Next Row* is, 1 short stitch into point, 3 chain, 1 treble into third treble, 3 chain, 1 treble into first chain, 3 chain, 1 treble into point. The *Next 4 Rows* are long stitch and chain into every other stitch. Then for the *Last Row,* 2 short stitches into first 3 holes, and only one into every fourth hole.

THE LUCILLE DOYLEY

Extract from *Fancy Needlework Illlustrated,* No. 14, 1910. This lace is easier than it appears. It is also suitable for a straight edge.

The edging measures 2 in. wide, and the damask centre 7 in. in diameter. Ardern's or Strutt's Crochet Cotton No. 30 should be used.

Begin with 8 chain, 1 treble into sixth chain, and 5 treble into next 2, turn with 5 chain, * 1 treble into second treble, 2 chain, 1 treble into fourth treble, 2 chain and 1 treble into sixth treble, 5 chain, 6 treble under 5 chain, 5 chain; turn and repeat from * until 4 points are done along one side, and 3 points and 6 treble on the other, then work 12 chain, 1 double crochet back into sixth (forming a loop), 10 chain, 1 double crochet into first point, 12 treble (3 chain for first) under loop of 10 chain, 1 double crochet into loop at the end; ** turn with 10 chain, 1 treble into seventh treble on first arm, 2 chain, and 1 treble in next treble to the end, making 5 treble; turn with 2 chain, 1 double crochet in next point, 2 chain, 1 double crochet in first loop (of 2 chain), *** 5 chain, 1 double crochet in next, repeat from *** twice, then 2 chain, 12 treble under arm as before, and 1 double crochet in

Illust. 55 The Lucille Doyley.

loop, and repeat from ** making 6 arms, then 6 double crochet under 6 chain, and finish point as usual.

In the second and succeeding scallops, catch the first picot (of 5 chain) to the last on preceding scallop. Also when making the fifth foundation point after a scallop, when turning catch to middle of sixth arm.

Footing:
First Row: 3 treble (3 chain for first) in first point, * 3 chain, 3 treble in next point, repeat from * then 3 chain, and join.
Second Row: 3 treble under 3 chain, 3 chain, and repeat all along, join and fasten off and sew to damask centre.

THE CALEDON DOYLEY

Extract from *Fancy Needlework Illlustrated,* No. 14, 1910. This is a straight edging which has been eased to fit its circle of linen. Notice that the fans are not all the same size, due to errors in counting.

Begin with 30 chain.

First Row: 1 treble in sixth chain from needle, * 3 chain, miss 3 chain, 1 treble into next chain, * repeat from * to * till end of chain, making 7 holes; turn.

Second Row: 3 chain (for 1 treble), 8 treble into first hole, 2 chain, 1 treble on next treble, 3 treble into space, 1 treble on next treble, 2 chain, 1 treble on next treble, 3 treble into space, 1 treble on next treble, 2 chain, 1 treble on next treble, 2 chain, 1 treble on third chain of last row; turn.

Third Row: 5 chain, 1 treble on second treble, * 3 chain, miss 2 stitches, 1 treble on next, 3 chain, miss 3 stitches, 1 treble on next treble, repeat from * once, 3 chain, 1 treble on next treble, ** 1 chain, and 1 treble on next treble,

Illust. 56 The Caledon Doyley.

and repeat from ** 7 times; turn.

Fourth Row: 5 chain, 1 treble on second treble, * 2 chain, 1 treble on next treble, repeat from * 7 times, ** 3 treble into space, 1 treble on next treble, 2 chain, 1 treble on next treble, repeat from ** once, 2 chain, 1 treble at end; turn.

Fifth Row: 5 chain, 1 treble on second treble, * 3 chain, miss 2 stitches, 1 treble on next, 3 chain, miss 3 stitches, 1 treble on next, repeat from * once, ** 3 chain, 1 treble on next treble, repeat from ** 8 times; turn.

Sixth Row: 3 chain, * 5 treble into next space, repeat from * 7 times, ** 2 chain, 1 treble in next treble, 3 treble into space, 1 treble on next treble, repeat from ** once, 2 chain, 1 treble on next treble, 2 chain, 1 treble at end; turn.

Seventh Row: 5 chain, 1 treble on second treble, * 3 chain, miss 2 stitches, 1 treble on next, 3 chain, miss 3 stitches, 1 treble on next, repeat from * once, 2 chain, 1 treble on next treble, ** 3 chain, miss 3 stitches, 1 treble on next treble, and repeat from ** 7 times; turn.

Eighth Row: 7 chain, 1 treble on next treble, * 4 chain, 1 treble on next treble, repeat from * 6 times, ** 2 chain, 1 treble on next treble, 3 treble in space, 1 treble on next treble, repeat from ** once, 2 chain, 1 treble on next treble, 2 chain, 1 treble at end; turn.

Ninth Row: 5 chain, 1 treble on next treble, * 3 chain, miss 2 stitches, 1 treble on next treble, 3 chain, miss 3 stitches, 1 treble on next treble, repeat from * once, 2 chain, 1 treble on next treble, then 5 treble into each of next 8 spaces; turn.

Tenth Row: 4 chain, 4 treble on 4 treble, 2 chain, * 5 treble on next 5 treble, 2 chain, repeat from * 5 times, 4 treble on next 4 treble, 2 chain, 1 treble on last treble of group, ** 2 chain, 1 treble on next treble, 3 treble in space, 1 treble on next treble, repeat from ** once, 2 chain, 1 treble on next treble, 2 chain, 1 treble at end; turn.

Eleventh Row: 5 chain, 1 treble on next treble, * 3 chain, miss 2 stitches, 1 treble on next treble, 3 chain, miss 3 stitches, 1 treble on next treble, repeat from * once, 2 chain, miss 2 chain and 1 treble, and work ** 2 treble, 2 chain, and 2 treble, into next space of 2 chain, 5 chain, and repeat from ** 8 times; turn.

Twelfth Row: 2 treble, 2 chain, and 2 treble in first space of 2 chain, * 1 chain, 1 double crochet into centre of the five chain of last row, 1 chain, 2 treble, 2 chain, and 2 treble, into next space, repeat from * 7 times, and finish as in tenth row with 2 chain, 5 treble, repeat once, 2 chain, 1 treble, 2 chain, 1 treble; turn.

Thirteenth Row: Begins like the eleventh, with 5 chain, 1 treble, * 3 chain, 1 treble, repeat from * 3 times, 2 chain, 2 treble, 2 chain and 2 treble in space in centre of group, ** 2 chain, 1 double crochet on double crochet, 2 chain, 2 treble, 2 chain, and 2 treble in next group, repeat from ** 7 times; turn.

Fourteenth Row: 3 chain, 2 treble, 2 chain and 2 treble in space in centre of group, 3 chain, 1 double crochet in double crochet, 3 chain, continue to end, finishing as in the tenth row.

Fifteenth Row: Like the eleventh, but along the Fan work 4 chain, 1 double crochet, and 4 chain, between groups.

Sixteenth Row: 3 chain, 2 treble, 5 chain, put needle through first chain to form a picot, 2 treble, 1 picot, and 2 treble, all in centre space of first group, * 5 chain, 1 double crochet on double crochet, 5 chain, 2 treble, 1 picot, 2 treble, 1 picot, 2 treble, 1 picot, and 2 treble in next group, * repeat 7 times, and finish like tenth row; turn.

Seventeenth Row: 5 chain, 1 treble, * 3 chain, 1 treble (as in former rows), repeat from * 3 times, 3 chain, 1 treble into treble besides picot, 5 chain, 1 double crochet into centre picot, 5 chain 1 double crochet into next picot; turn.

Repeat from the second to seventeenth rows for lace, catching back on to previous Fan, (i.e., catch back to previous Fan when turning at second, fourth, sixth, eighth and tenth rows).

FAN LACE

Extract from *The Craft of the Crochet Hook*, edited by Flora Klickmann, 1912. This is a complicated pattern, only suitable for experienced workers.

14 ch, join in ring.
1st Row: 3 ch, 32 tr, join with sl st.
2nd Row: 5 ch, miss 3, 1 dc in next, repeat 7 times.
3rd Row: 2 sl st, 2 dc; 1dc, 1 picot, 1dc in same stitch, 2 dc, * 12 ch, fasten back in 3rd stitch before picot, into loop work 1 dc, 1 h tr, 4 tr, 3 l tr, 1 picot, 3 l tr, * repeat from * to * twice. 12 ch, fasten back in 3rd before picot, into

Illust. 57 The Fan Lace.

loop 1 dc, 1 h tr, 4 tr, 1 l tr, 1 picot, 2 l tr, 1 picot, 2 l tr, 1 picot, 1 l tr, 4 tr, 1 h tr, 1 dc, 1 sl st, fill in the other 3 leaves with 4 tr, 1 h tr, 1 dc, 1 sl st in each leaf. ** 5 ch, miss 4 dc, 2dc; . 1 dc, 1 picot, 1dc in next stitch, 2 dc, 12 ch, fasten back in 3rd stitch before picot, into loop 1dc, 1 h tr, 2 tr, 5 ch, 1 sl st over ch between, 3 dc on 5 ch, 3 ch, sl st in 3rd tr of 1st leaf opposite, over ch, 1 dc, 1 picot, 1 dc, 5 ch, 1 dc, 1 picot, 1 dc over next ch, * 1 sl st into 3rd tr of leaf, continue leaf with 2 tr, 3 l tr, 1 picot, 3 l tr, 12 ch, fasten back in 3rd stitch before picot, into loop 1 dc, 1 h tr, 2 tr, * 8 ch, 1 sl st over ch between, 4 dc over 8 ch, 6 ch, sl st into 2nd tr of opposite leaf, over ch 2 dc, 1 picot, 2 dc, 6 ch, over next ch 2 dc, 1 picot, 2 dc.
Repeat from * to *, 10 ch, 1 sl st over ch between, 5 dc over 10 ch, 6 ch, sl st into 2nd tr of opposite leaf, over ch 3 dc, 1 picot, 3 dc, 6 ch over next ch, 3 dc, 1 picot, 3 dc.
Repeat from * to *, 11 ch, sl st over ch between, 11 ch, sl st on 2nd tr of leaf opposite, over ch 3 dc, 1 picot, 3 dc, 1 picot between, 4 dc, 9 ch, fasten back into 3rd dc after picot, into loop 5 dc, 1 picot, 5 dc, finish other loop with 3 dc, 1 picot, 3 dc.
Sl st into 3rd tr of leaf, continue leaf with 2 tr, 1 l tr, 1 picot, 2 l tr, 1 picot, 2 l tr, 1 picot, 1 l tr, 4 tr, 1 h tr, 1 dc, 1 sl st, finish other leaves with 4 tr, 1 h tr, 1 dc, 1 sl st in each leaf. **
Repeat from * to ** 4 times for straight lace and 5 times for corner, joining fans as in illustration.

To make 8 raised points in centre:
1 dc into the tr into which the dc of 2nd Row was worked, 5 ch, repeat 7 times, 1 sl st, 6 tr, 1 sl st into each 5 ch.

Heading:
1st Row: ** Begin on 2nd tr from picot, * 3 tr, 3 ch, * repeat from * to * on 4 leaves, 2 triple tr between leaf and point, 3 ch, 3 tr on 2 points of centre, 3 ch, 2 triple tr between, 3 ch. **
Repeat from ** to ** for length required.
For Corner:
2 triple tr, 1 dc, 2 triple tr.
2nd Row: dc on tr, 3 dc over ch between.

FILET EDGING

Extract from *Beautiful Crochet on Household Linen,* edited by Flora Klickmann, 1916. This pattern uses an unusual notation for filet crochet.
0 = open mesh (usually called a space), S = solid mesh (usually called a block). 30, for example, means 3 open meshes.

Illust. 58 The Filet Edging.

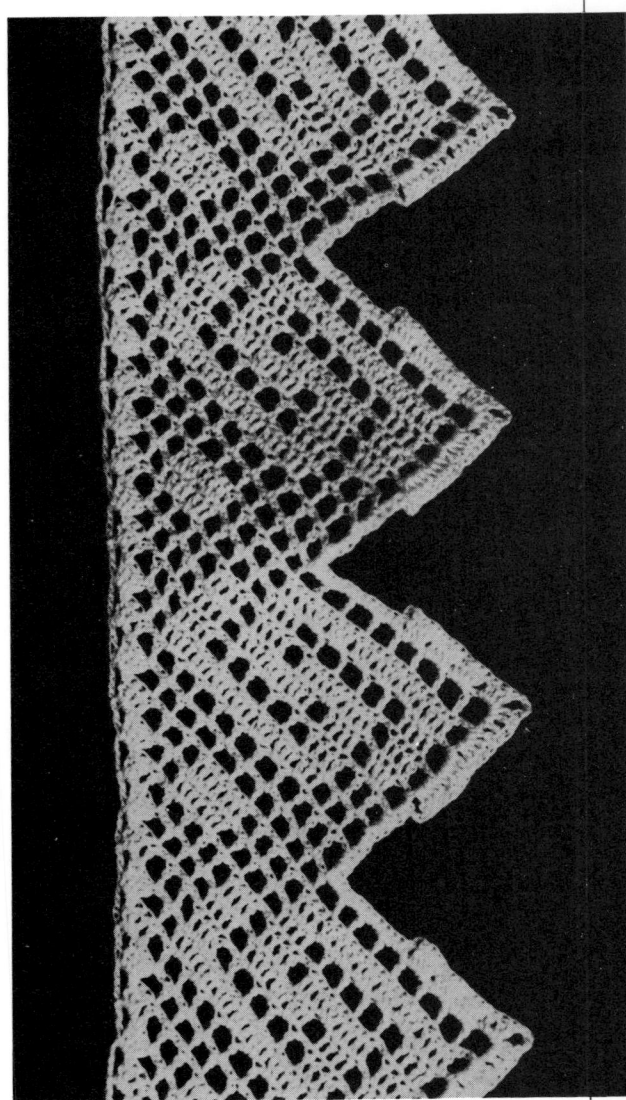

HERITAGE CROCHET: AN ANALYSIS

Work 37 ch, 6 ch to turn, 4 tr into next 4 ch, and 11 open spaces on to chain, 6 ch to turn.

2nd Row: 30, 7S, 20, in end space 4 tr, 3 ch, 1 tr.

3rd Row: Turn with 6 ch, 4 tr in first space, 30, 1S, 50, 1S, 30.

4th Row: 10, 1S, 10, 1S, 10, 3S, 10, 1S, 40, 4 tr, 3 ch, 1tr.

5th Row: 6 ch, 4 tr, 50, 1S, 10, 1S, 10, 3S, 10, 1S, 10.

6th Row: 10, 1S, 50, 1S, 40, 2S, 20, 4 tr, 3 ch, 1 tr.

7th Row: 6 ch, 4 tr, 30, 2S, 40, 7S, 10.

8th Row: 180, 4 tr, 3 ch, 1 tr.

This ends the point, commence again at 1st Row.

For the final edge, put in the tip space, 3 tr, 4 ch, 3 tr; 4 tr in each of next 3 spaces, each side, 3 ch, and 3 dc in each of the 4 spaces left each side.

PART TWO
TECHNICAL ANALYSIS

And don't imagine you can write like Dante,
Dive like your nephew, crochet like your auntie.
W.H. Auden, *Letter to Lord Byron,*
The Oxford Book of Satirical Verse, 1980

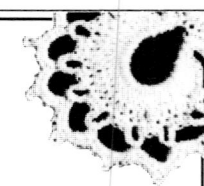

9
SOME OLD TECHNIQUES

FOUNDATION CHAINS

Were seldom counted accurately, but were overestimated, and any excess chain left unused. It would later be cut to within an inch or so, and unpicked to yield an end. It is not unusual to find excess foundation chains left dangling from old samples.

CIRCULAR MOTIFS

Were not always started with a ring of chain stitches, as is usual nowadays. Often the thread was wrapped a few times around the tip of a finger, or around a pencil or similar implement, and the resultant bundle of threads were slip-stitched together to form a foundation ring. The aperture could be adjusted by pulling the end of thread after the first round was worked.

FILET CROCHET EDGINGS

When worked widthways for a cloth, often needed a join between beginning and end. In order to avoid a thickened seam, the initial foundation chain was worked with a separate thread which could be unpicked afterwards. The free trebles of the first row were then caught into place invisibly with an end of thread from the final row. An alternative method was to replace the separate foundation chain with a cord, which was later withdrawn. Both methods need care, as the trebles when released tend to enjoy their freedom and become untwisted.

DAMASK DOYLEY CENTRES

Could once be purchased ready machine-hemmed in a range of sizes, but the feather-stitch hem was a favourite method for hand finishing. A plate or saucer of the approximate size was used as a template, and a circle marked on the linen with a pencil. The foot or inner edge of the crochet was whipped into place, and the fabric afterwards cut, allowing a small double hem. The hem was tacked into position on the wrong side, and feather-stitched from the right side. A soft embroidery cotton gives better results than a hard crochet cotton.

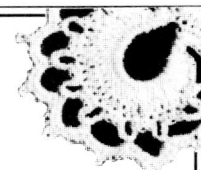

10
SELECTED
PATTERNS

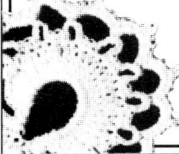

The pattern diagrams which follow are intended for experienced workers only, as a good general knowledge of techniques is essential. Measurements are not given because it is impossible exactly to identify the threads originally used. Hence it is advisable to try a pattern in different sizes of thread before embarking on a major project.

KEY TO THE SYMBOLS USED

Symbol	Stitch, etc.	Abbreviation
O	chain	ch
⌒	slip stitch	ss
I	double crochet	dc
│	half treble	htr
†	treble	tr
‡	double treble	dtr
‡	triple treble	ttr

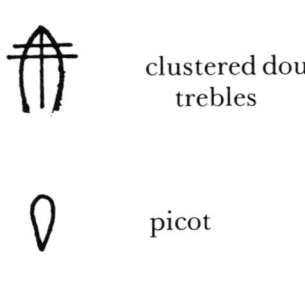

consecutive double crochet

consecutive trebles

treble shell

clustered double trebles

picot

start

direction of work

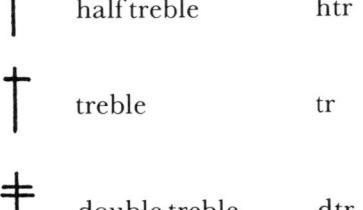

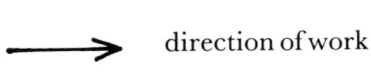

The symbols on each diagram are connected by a continuous line which indicates the sequence of work.

65

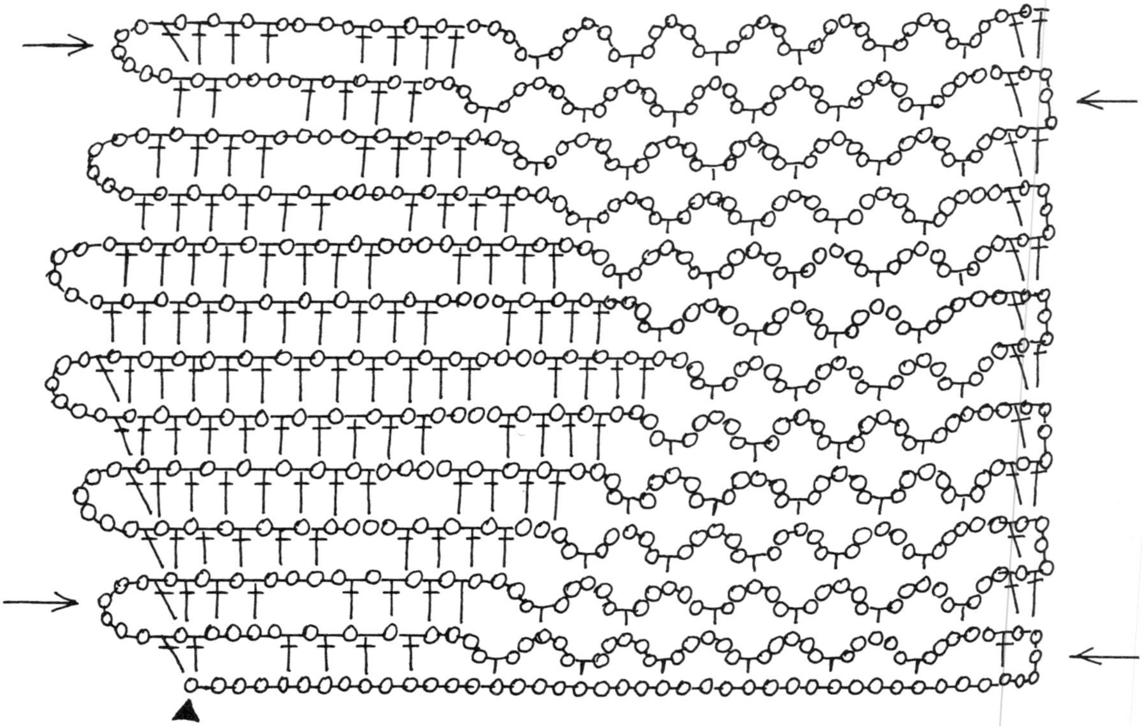

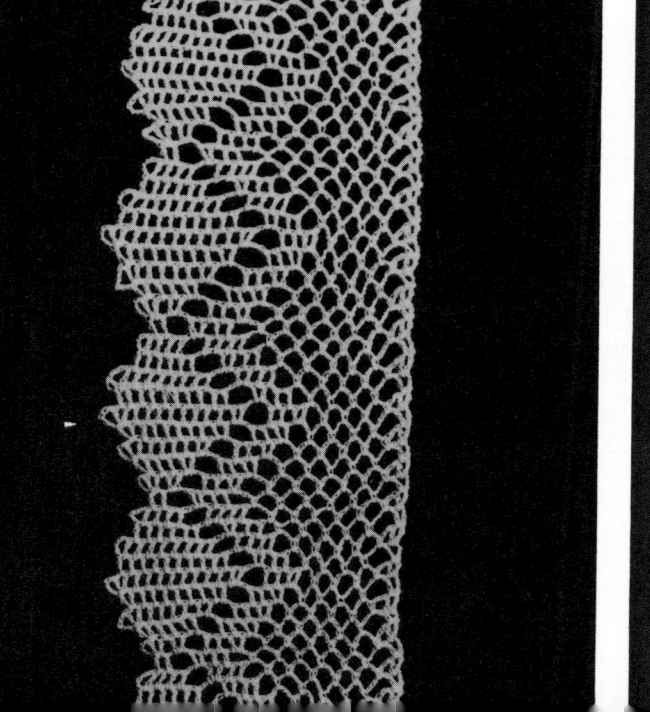
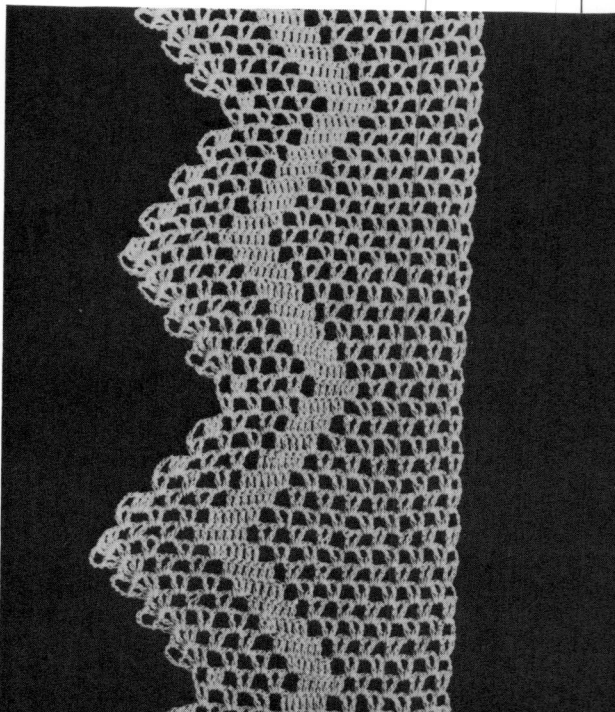

Illust. 59 Edging in torchon crochet. Weldon's Practical Needlework *gave a prototype in 1892.*

▲*Illust. 59a Start with 44 ch and work the first tr into the 6th ch from the hook.*

SELECTED PATTERNS

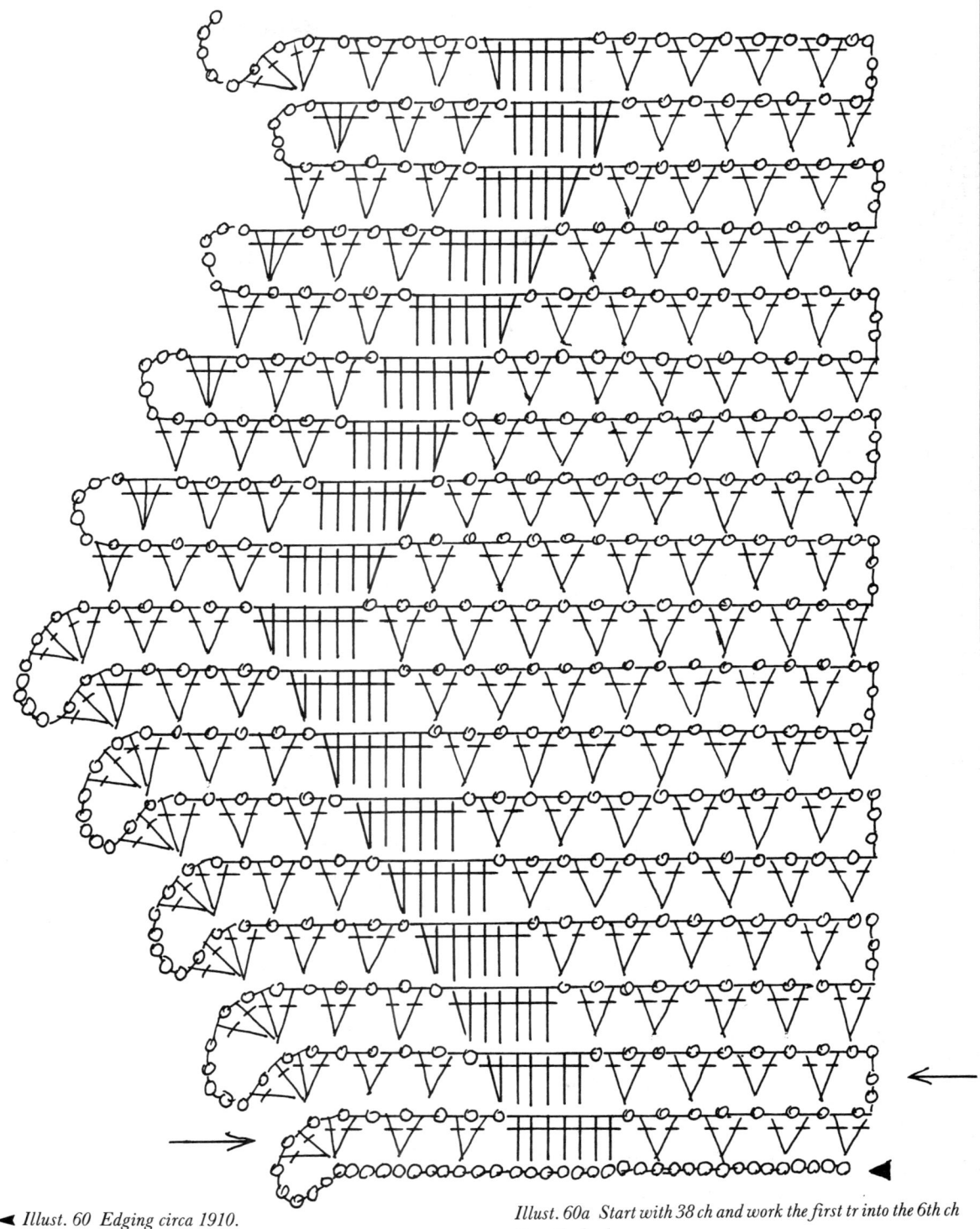

◄ *Illust. 60 Edging circa 1910.*

Illust. 60a Start with 38 ch and work the first tr into the 6th ch from the hook.

Illust. 61 A prototype of the left-hand design appeared in ➤
Weldon's Practical Needlework *in 1892.*

Illust. 61a(i) – There are 19 tr plus the turning ch to each fan.

SELECTED PATTERNS

Illust. 61a(ii) – There are 8 groups of clustered dtr to each repeat.

Illust. 62 These little edgings will adapt to a curve. ➤

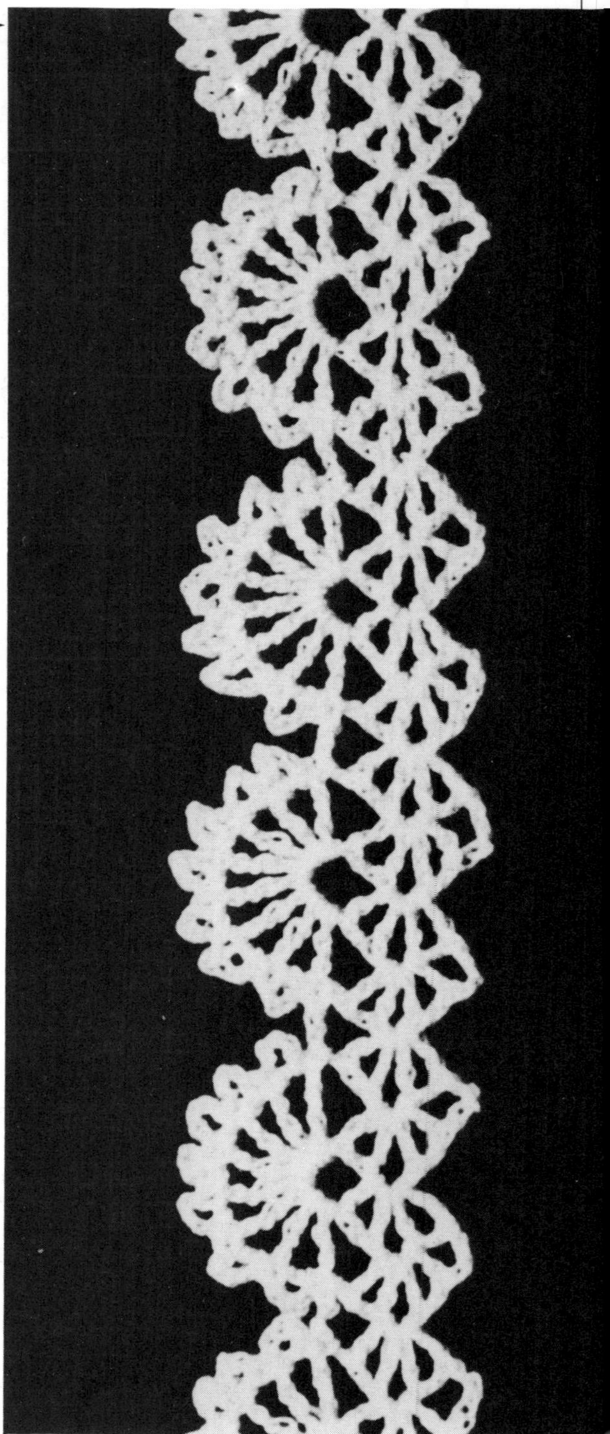

Illust. 62a(i) – The braid is worked widthways and the fans are worked lengthways.

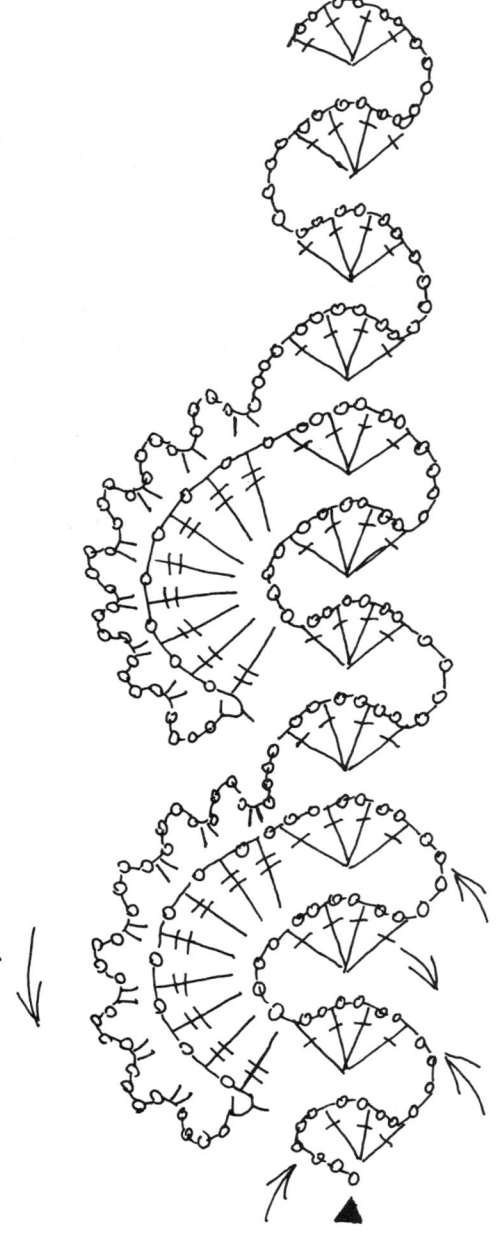

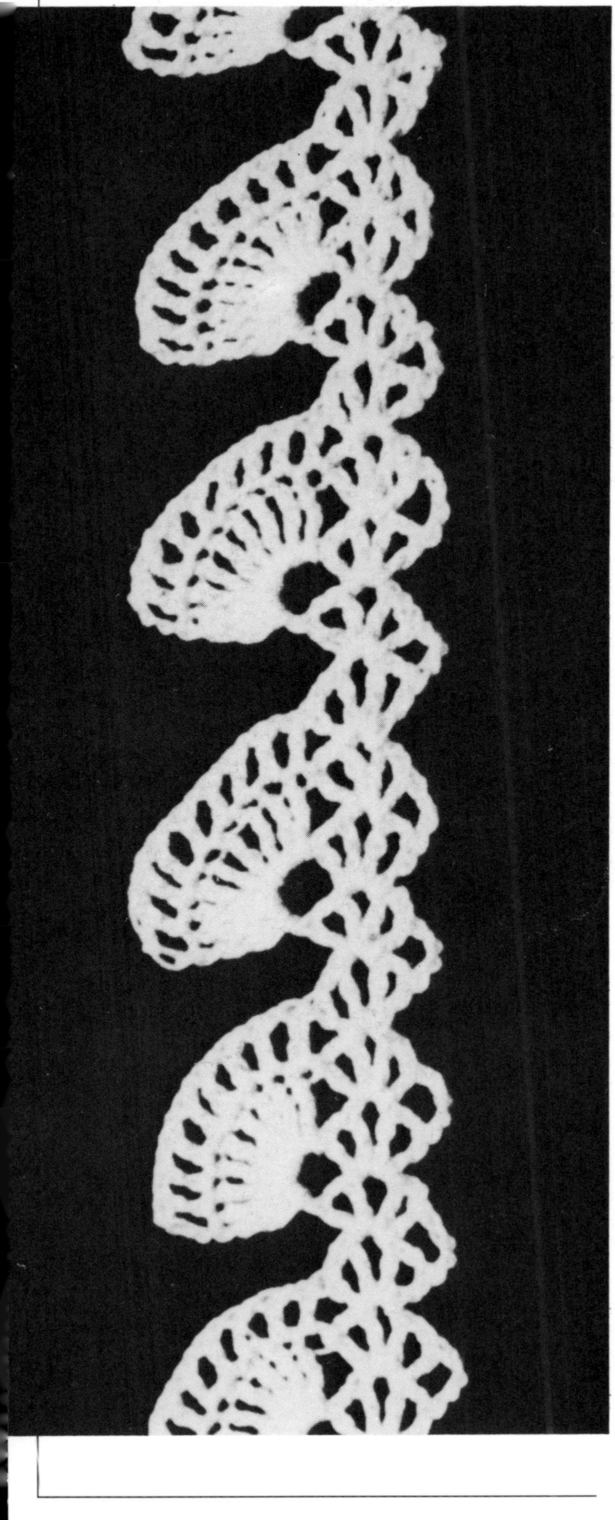

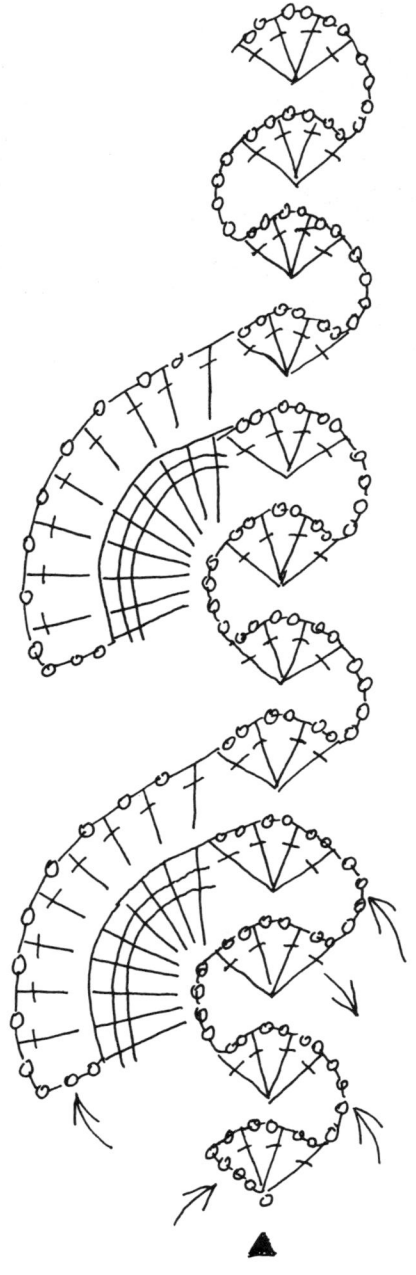

Illust. 62a(ii) – A variation with unconnected fans.

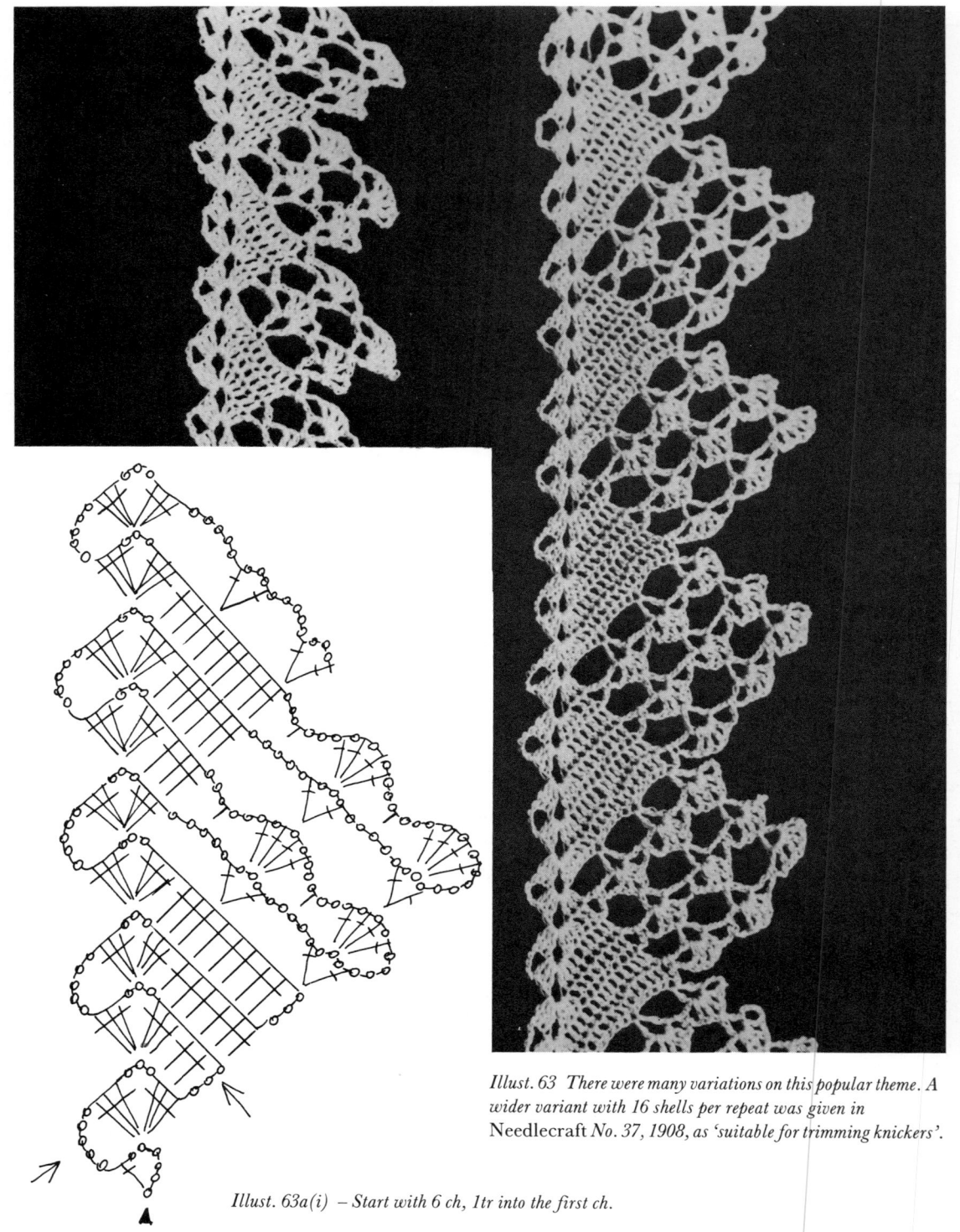

Illust. 63 There were many variations on this popular theme. A wider variant with 16 shells per repeat was given in Needlecraft No. 37, 1908, as 'suitable for trimming knickers'.

Illust. 63a(i) – Start with 6 ch, 1tr into the first ch.

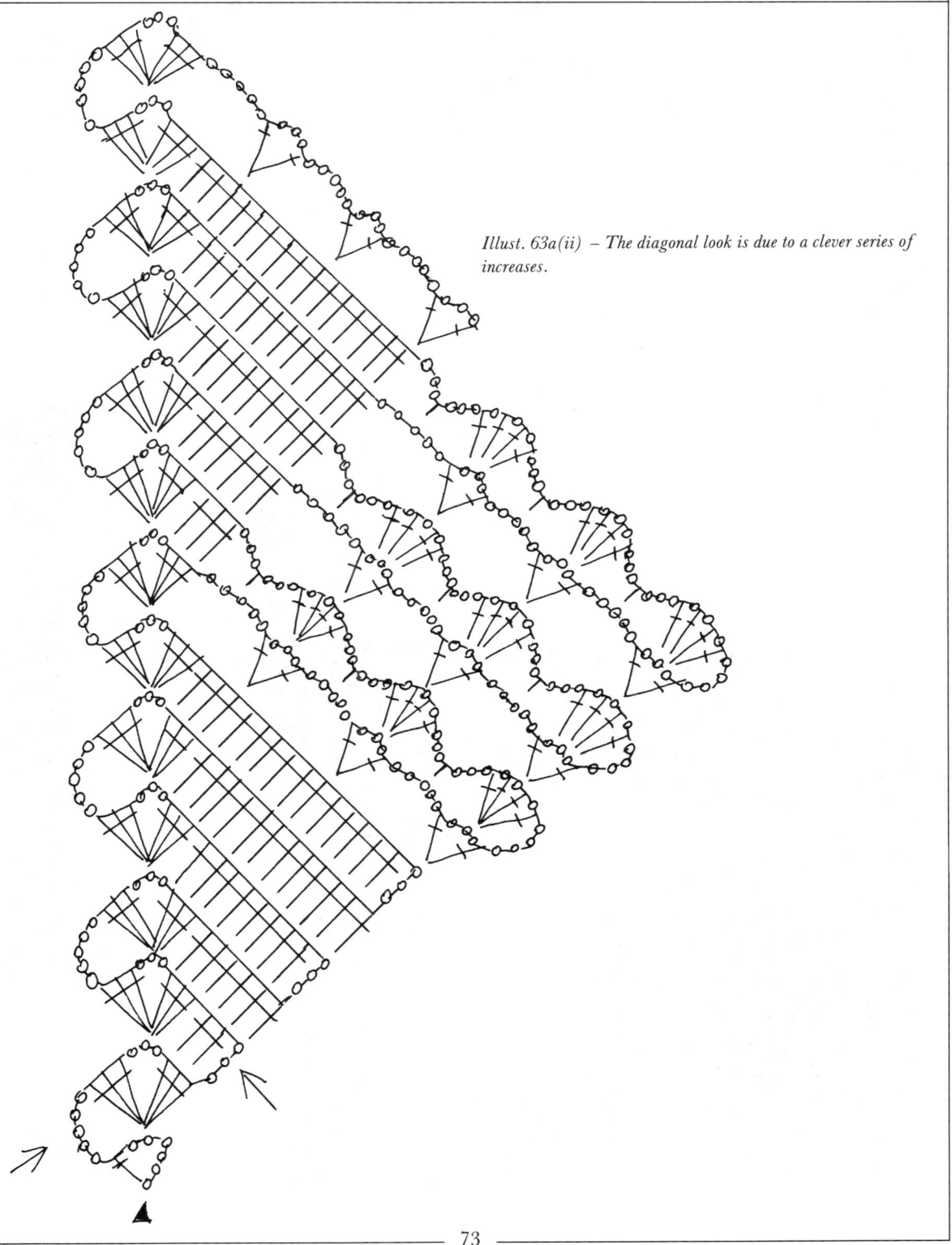

Illust. 63a(ii) – The diagonal look is due to a clever series of increases.

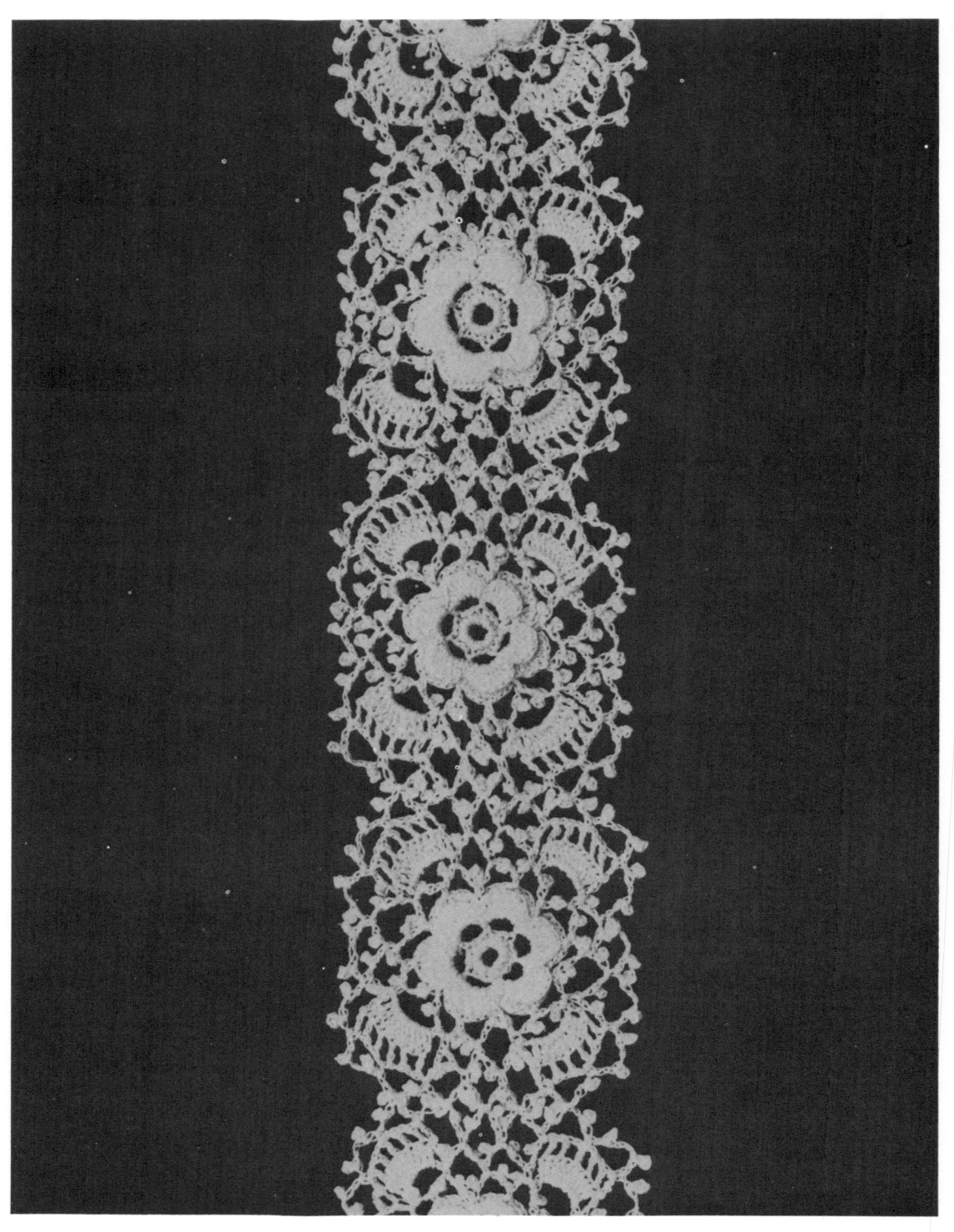

◄*Illust. 64 Irish baby crochet – the* Rose and Crown *motif.*

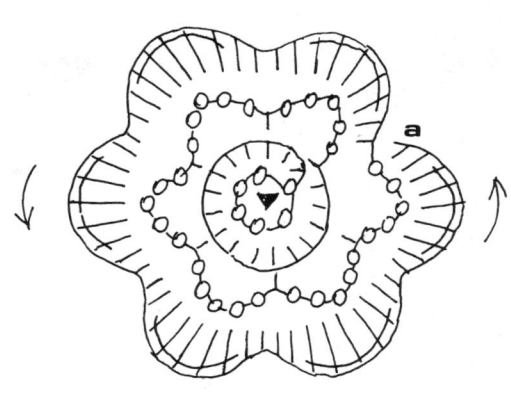

*Illust. 64a The central roses are double layered. Work to 'a'
then continue from 'b'. Each ss of the 4th round is worked into
the dc of the 2nd round. For the picots work 5 ch, ss to first of
5 ch.*

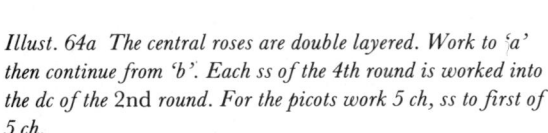

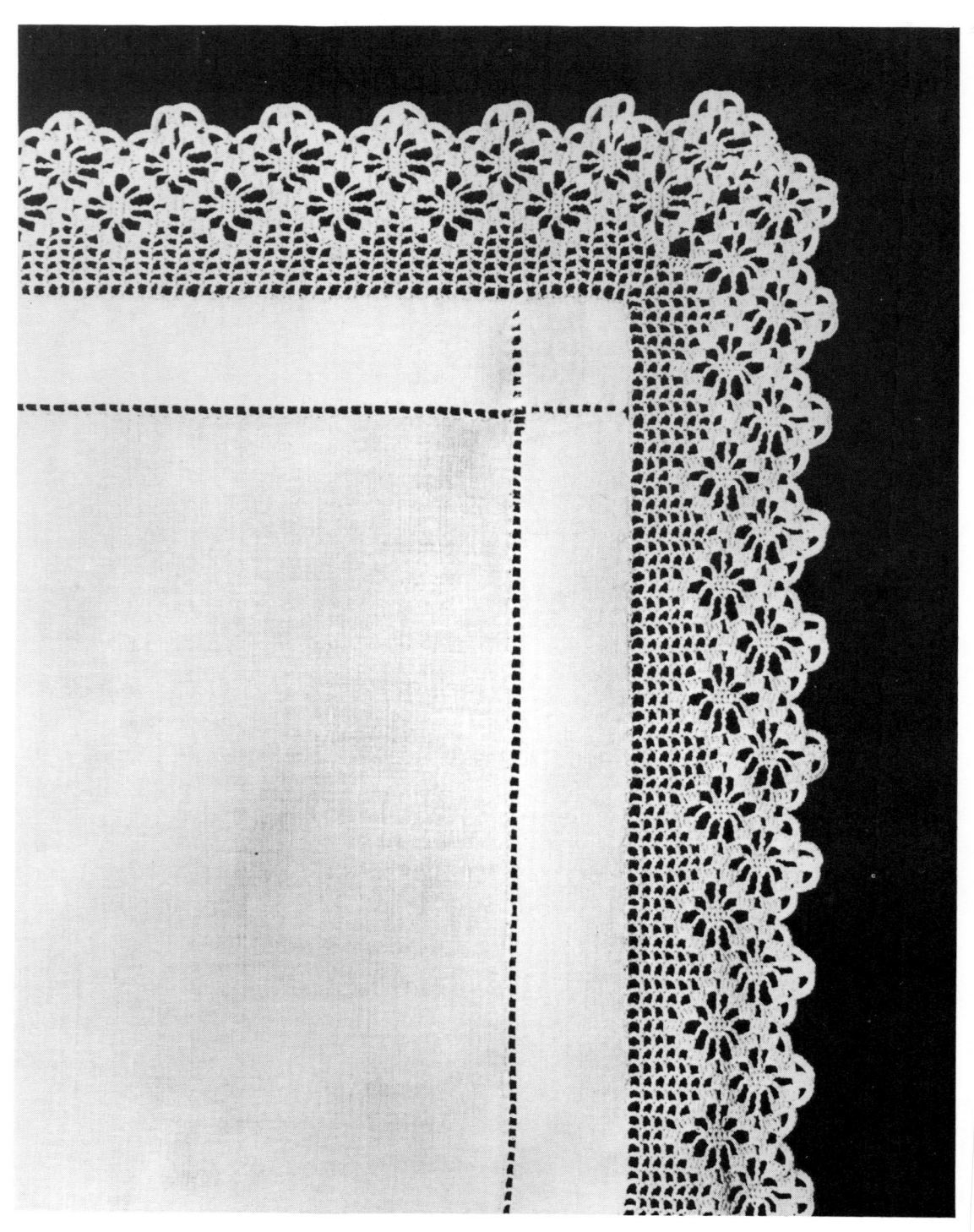

◄*Illust. 65* Torchon Spider *formation with a filet mesh.*

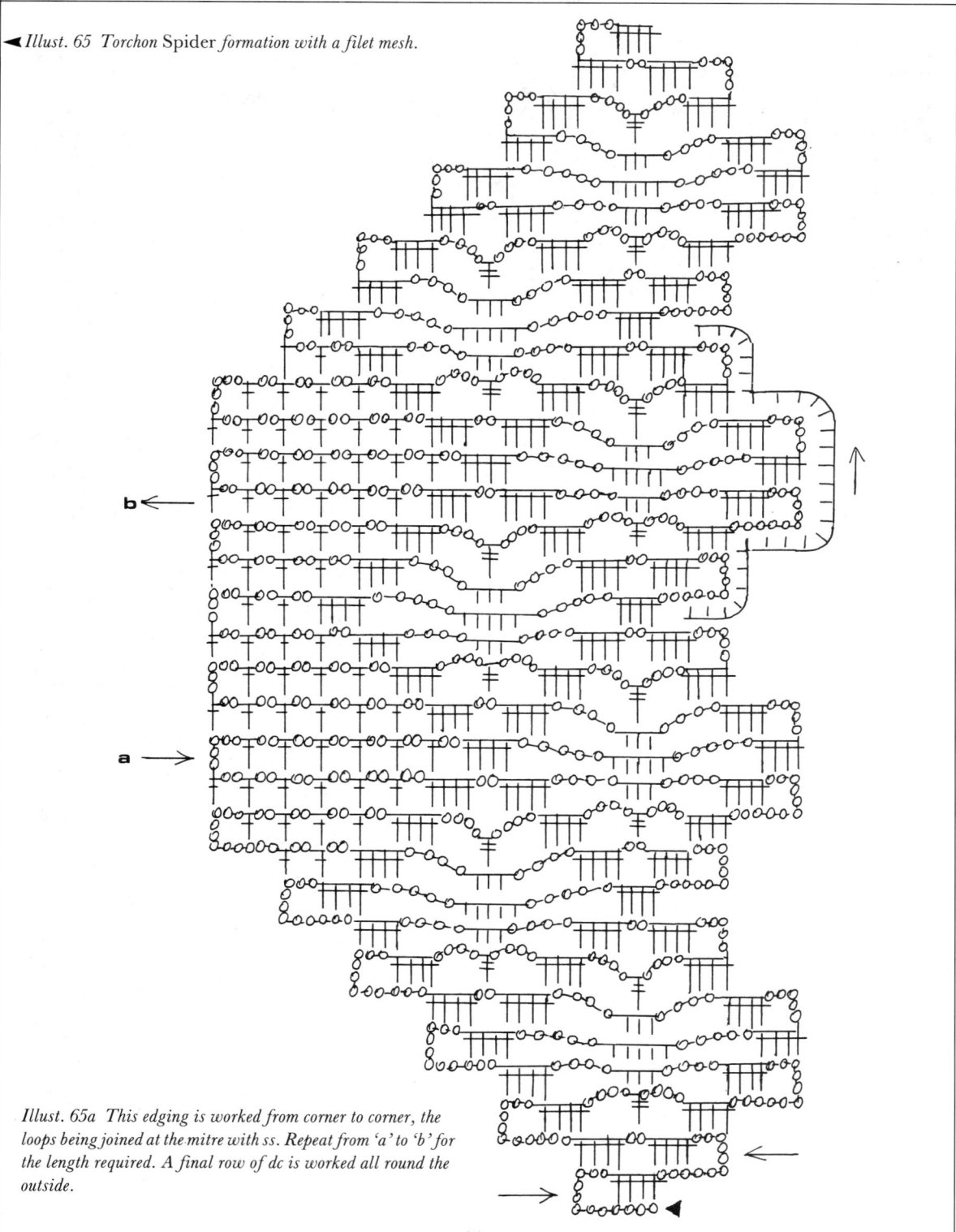

Illust. 65a This edging is worked from corner to corner, the loops being joined at the mitre with ss. Repeat from 'a' to 'b' for the length required. A final row of dc is worked all round the outside.

Illust. 66a(i) Start with 61 ch, plus 3 ch to turn. ➤

Illust. 66 Filet guipure crochet with lacet mesh, from
Weldon's Practical Needlework *No. 230, 1905*

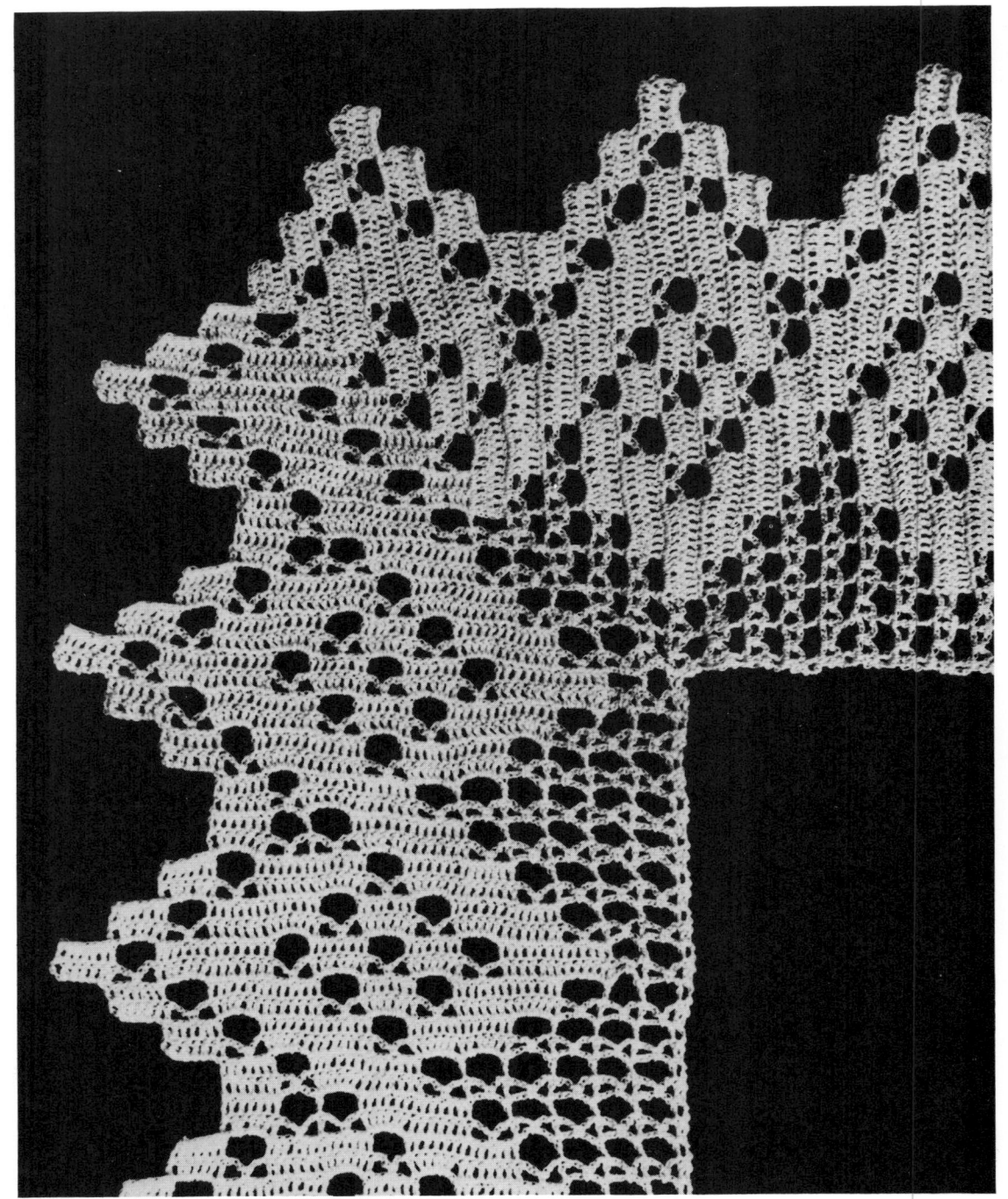

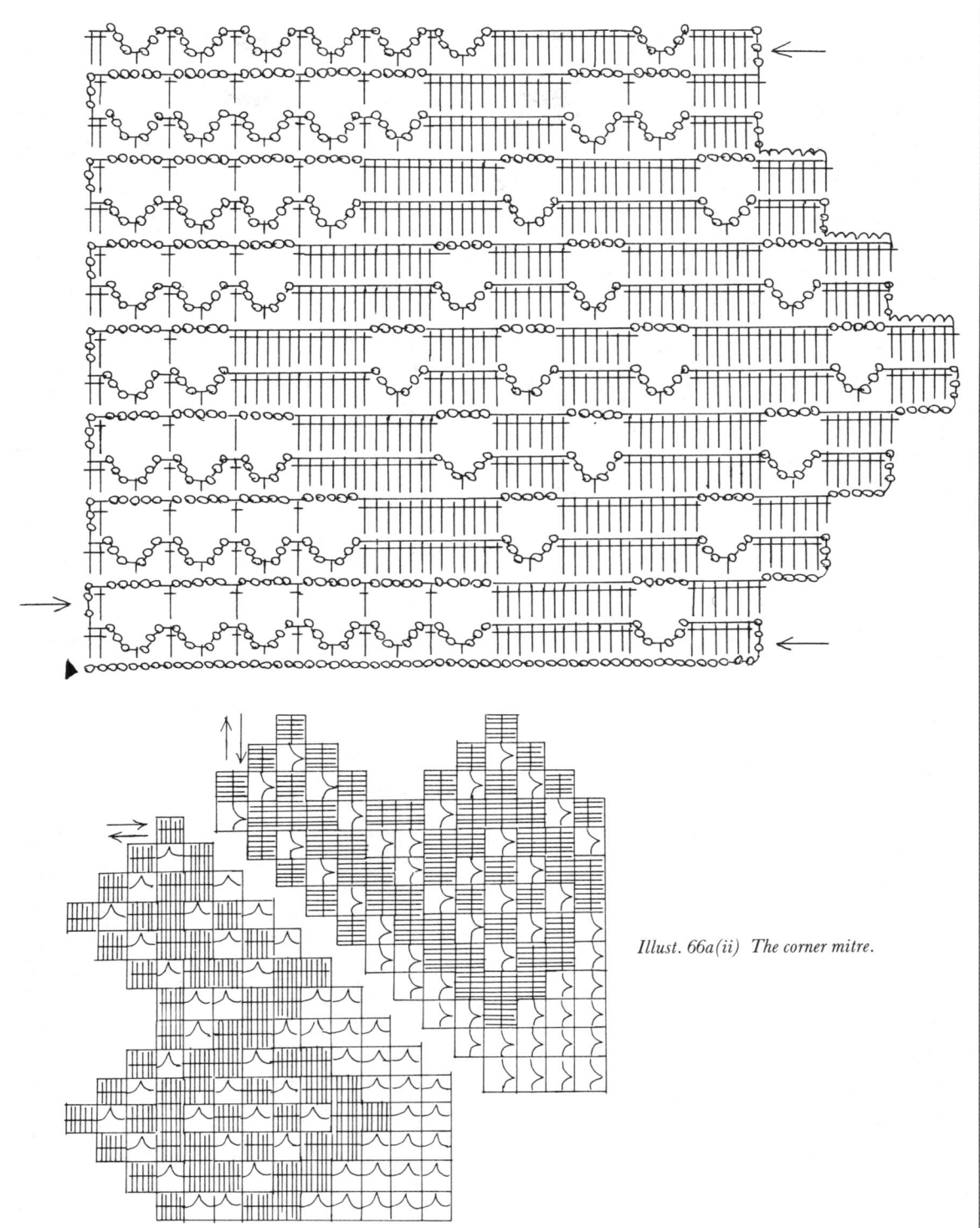

Illust. 66a(ii) The corner mitre.

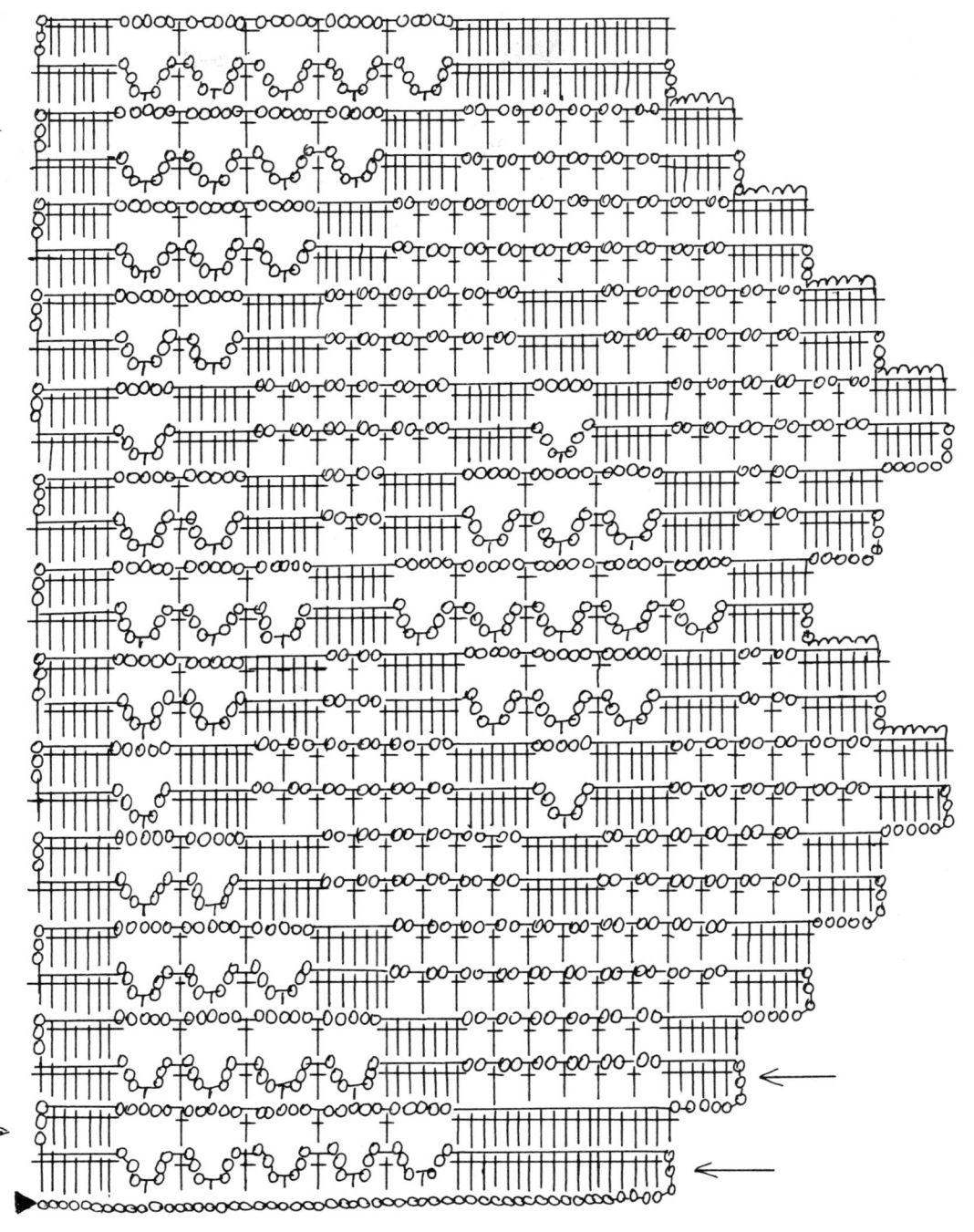

◄ *Illust. 67 Edging and insertion in filet guipure crochet, circa 1912.*

Illust. 67a(i) Start with 55 ch, plus 3 ch to turn.

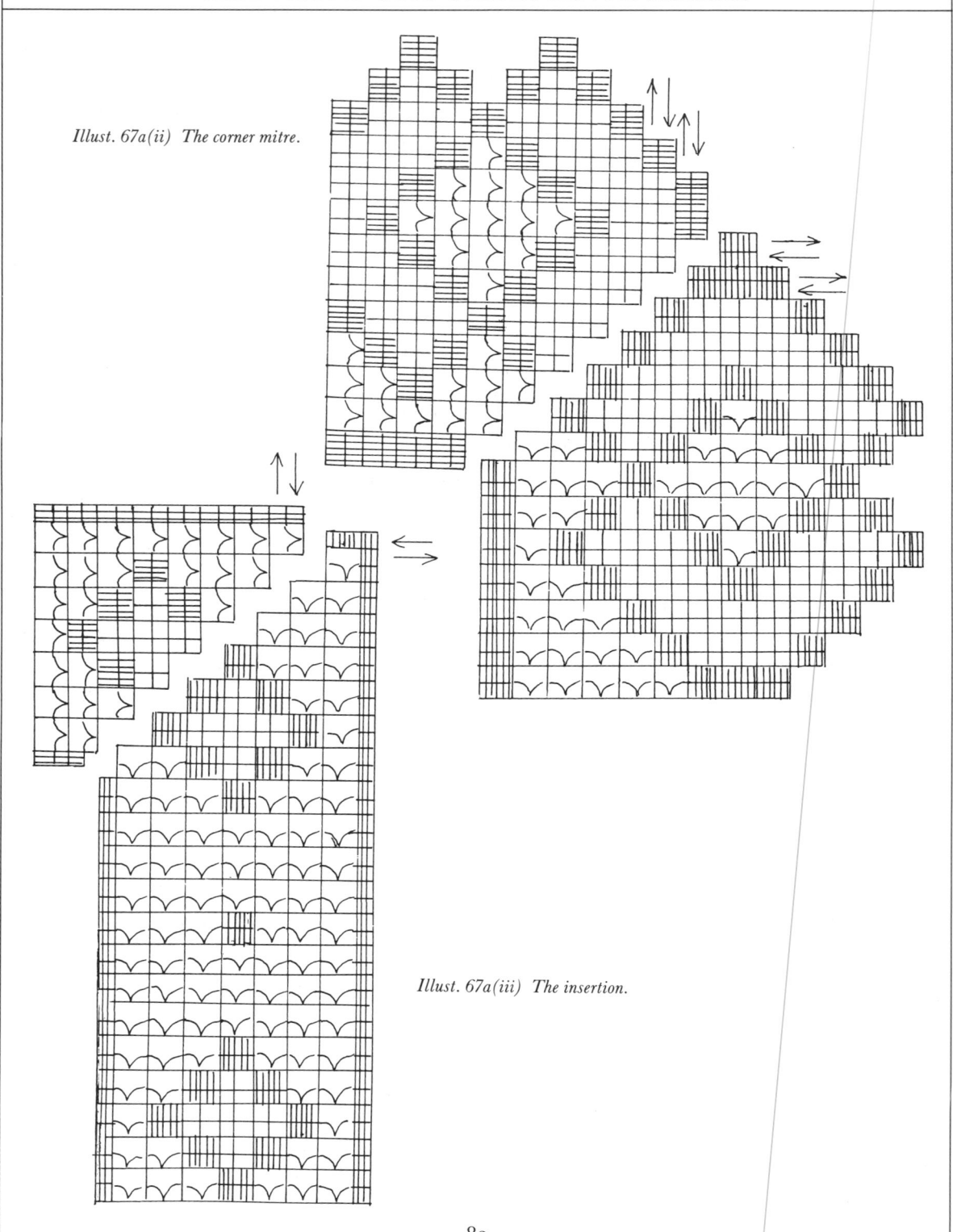

Illust. 67a(ii) The corner mitre.

Illust. 67a(iii) The insertion.

*Illust. 68 Lace-makers will recognise the inspiration of this ►
design as the torchon* Fir-Tree Fan, *faithfully copied here in
crochet.*

*Illust. 68a Start with 288 ch and work in rounds. For the picots
work 3 ch, ss to top of dtr (or ttr).*

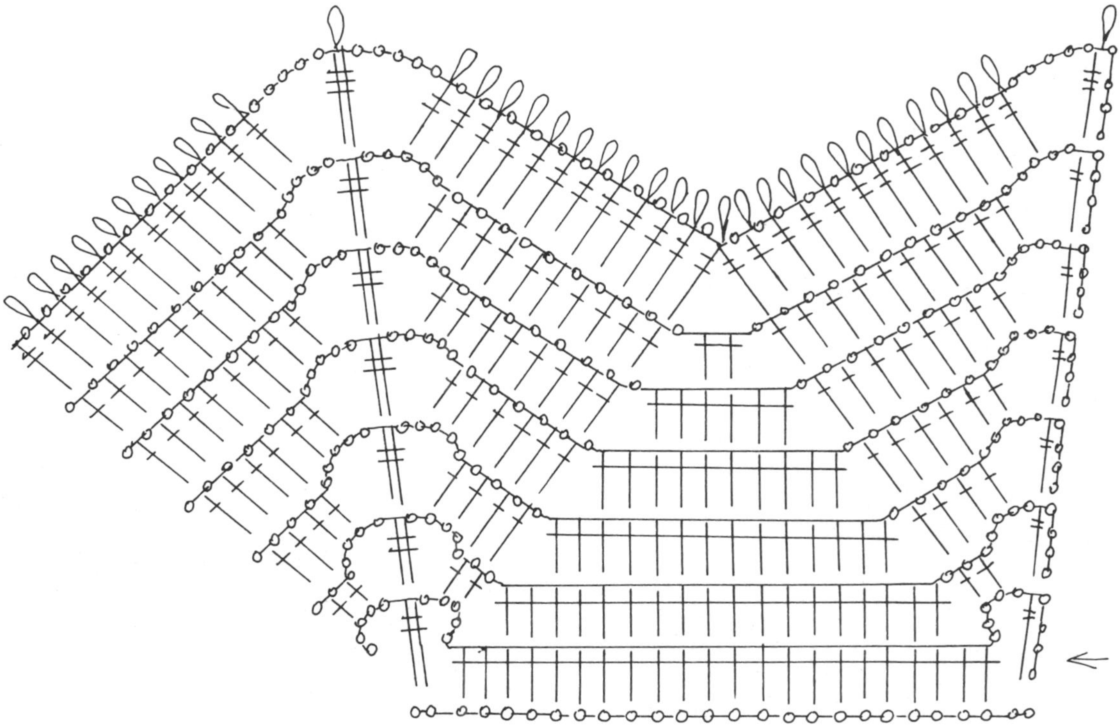

◄ *Illust. 69 A complicated fan design.*

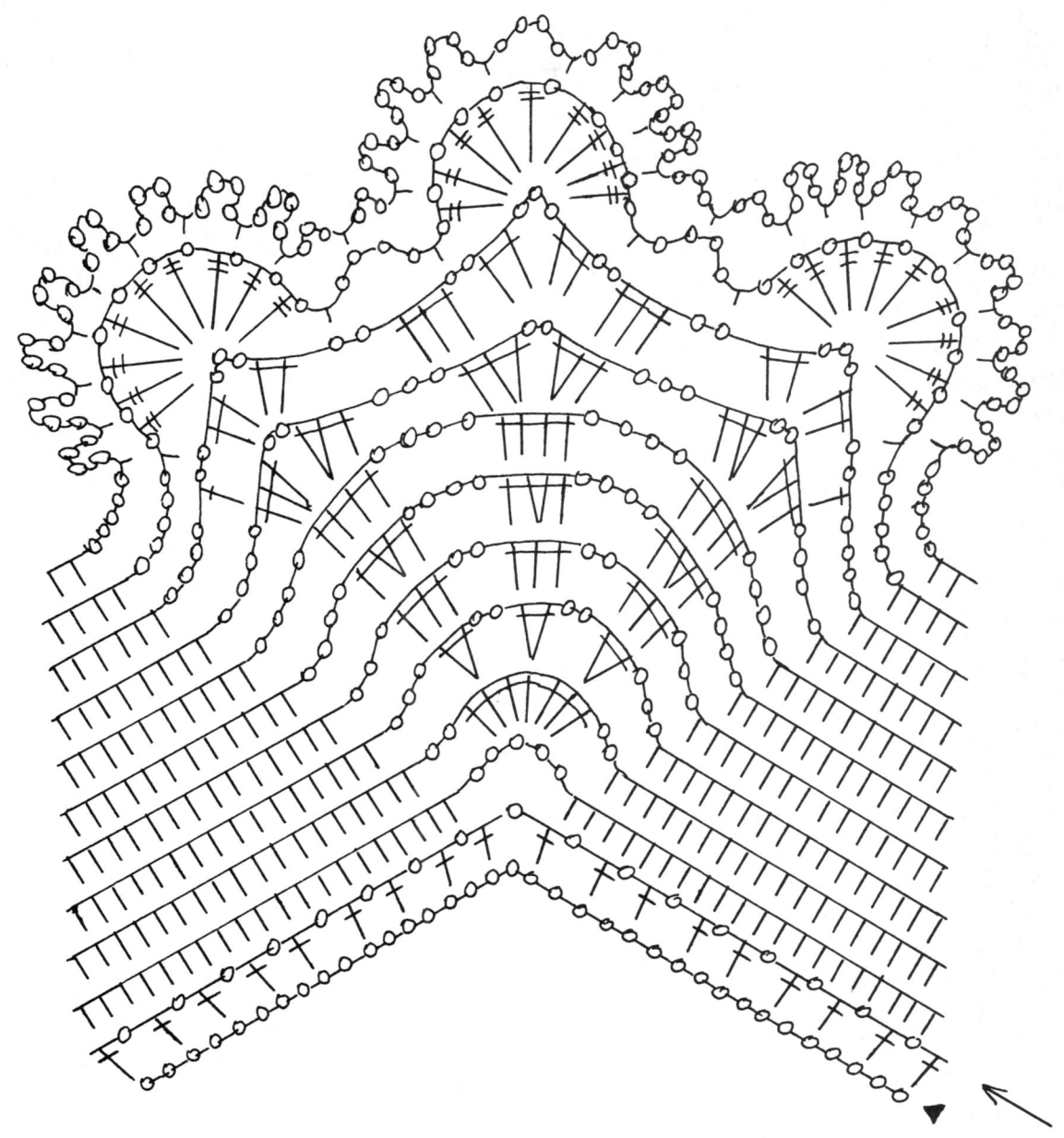

Illust. 69a Start with 162 ch and work in rounds. There are 20 dc at the base of each triangle.

Illust. 70 There were a multitude of variations on this Feather and Fan *theme. It is an elaboration of the shell counting patterns which so often featured in old shawls.*

Illust. 70a Start with 120 ch and work in rounds. For the picots ➤ *work 4 ch, ss to top of tr.*

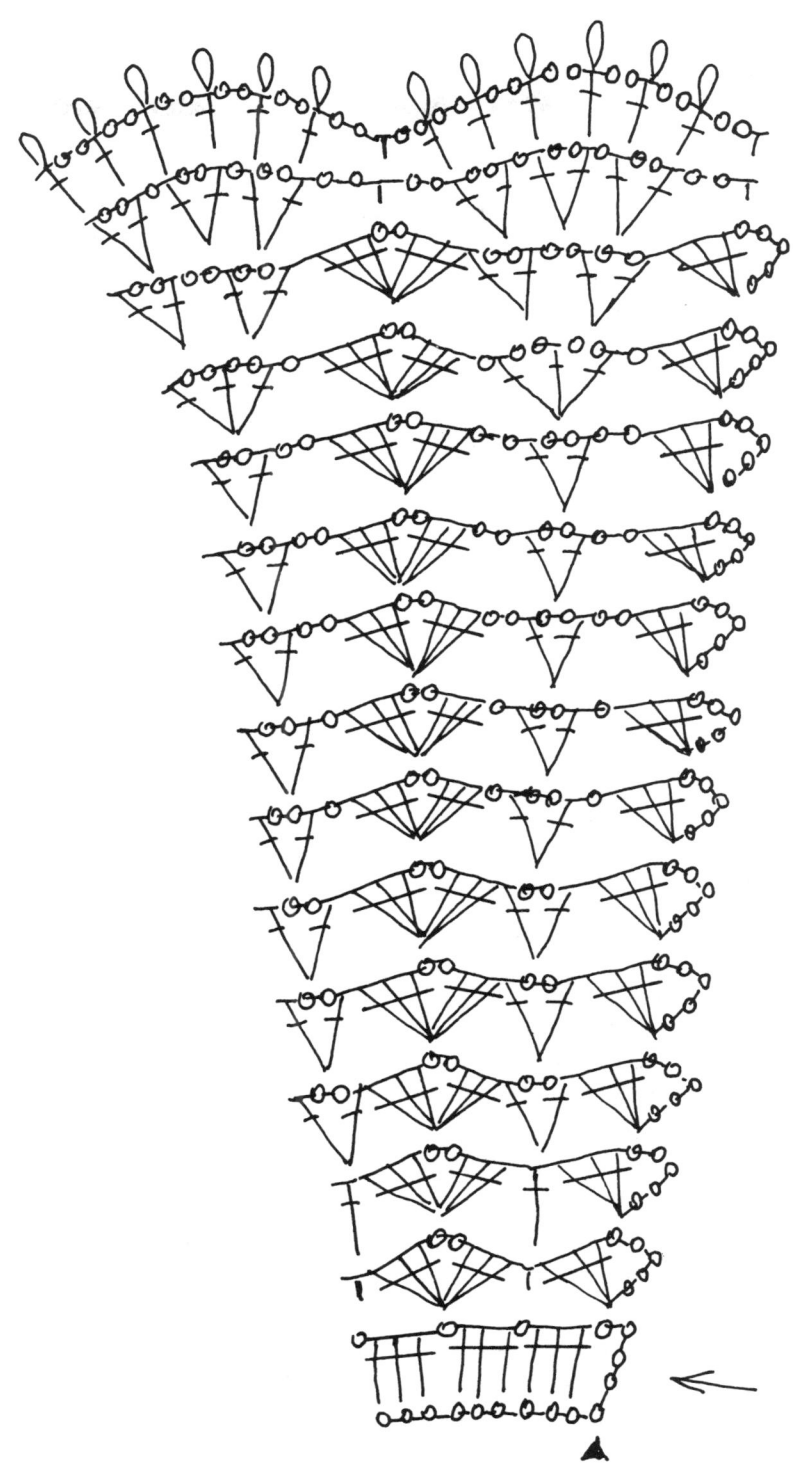

Illust. 71 Edging in Irish baby crochet showing the treble ▶
'crown'.

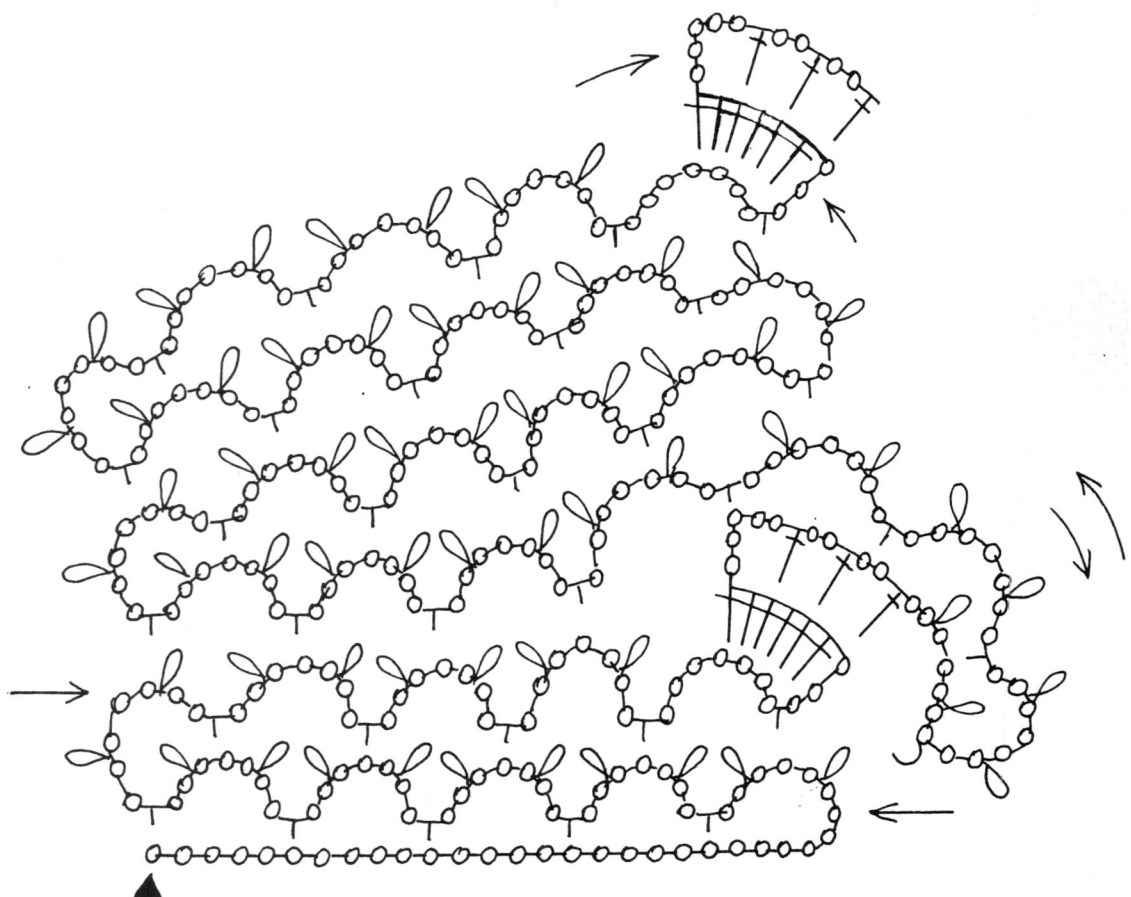

Illust. 71a For the picots work 5 ch, ss to first of 5 ch.

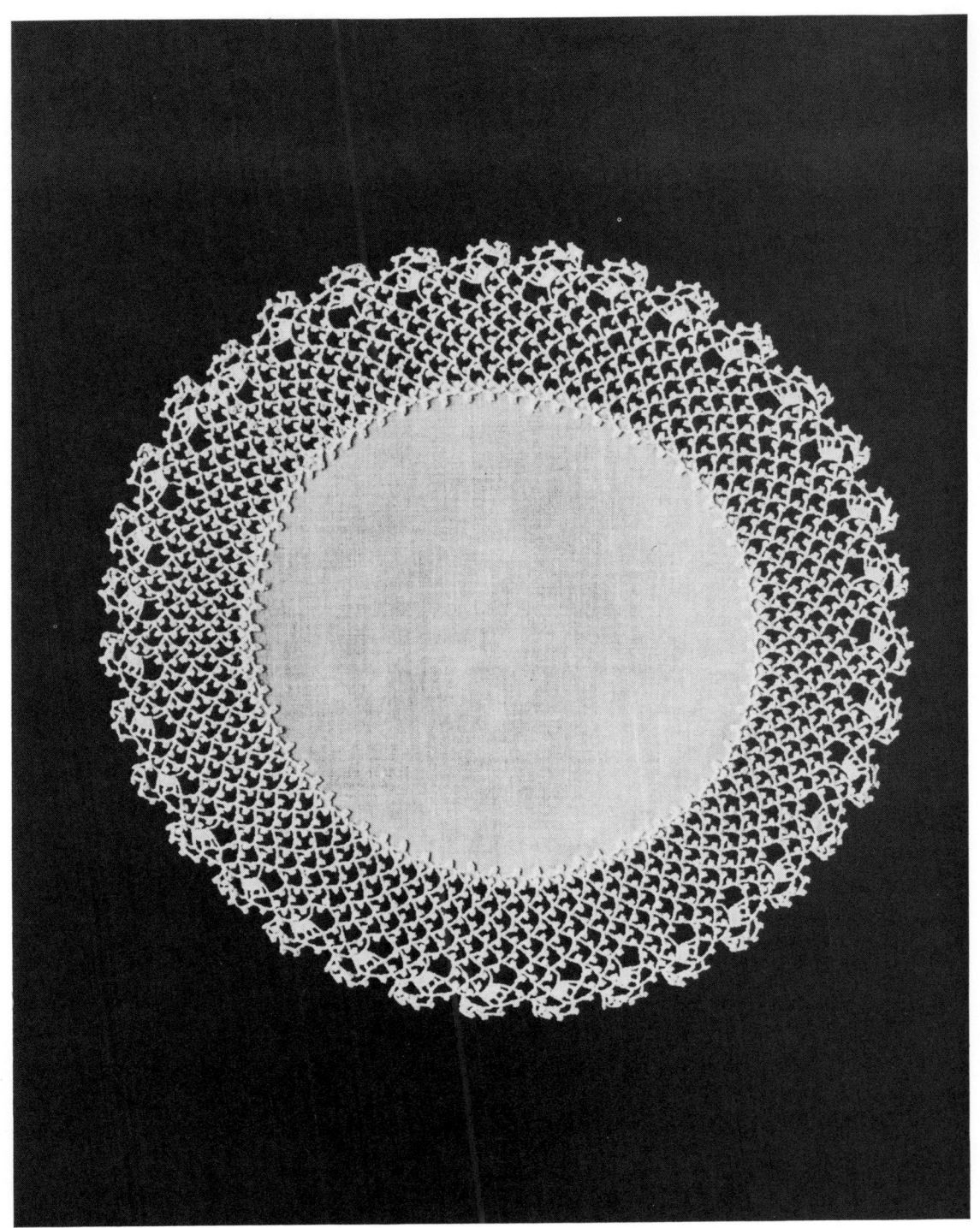

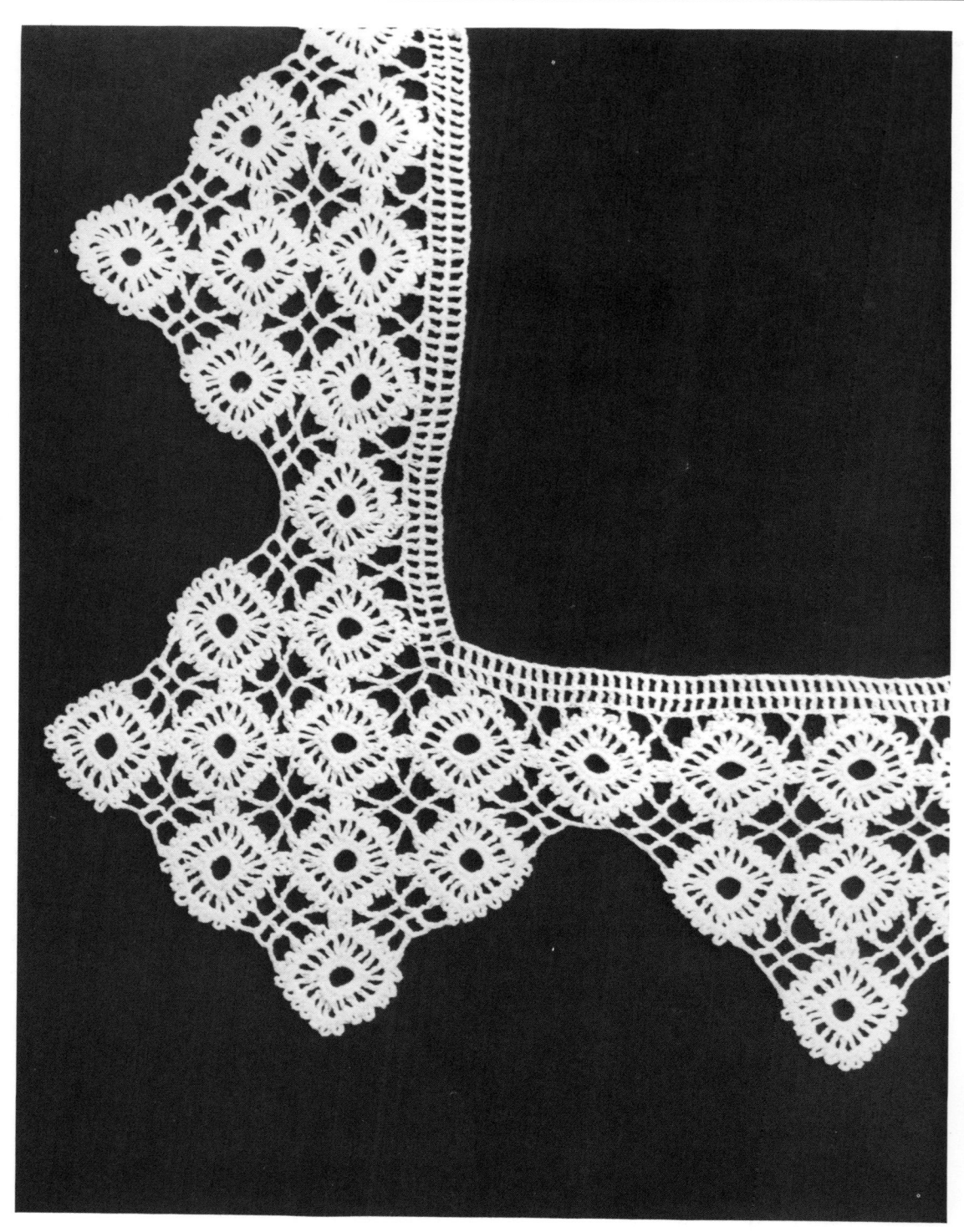

SELECTED PATTERNS

◄*Illust. 72 The fillings which connect these motifs are very cleverly arranged.*

Illust. 72a Make the motifs first, joining them as shown. To work the forked quadruple treble, place 4 'overs' on the hook, insert the hook into the appropriate loop, work off 2 of the 'overs' only, place 2 more 'overs' on the hook, insert the hook into the appropriate loop and work off these 2 'overs' plus the original 2 which remain.

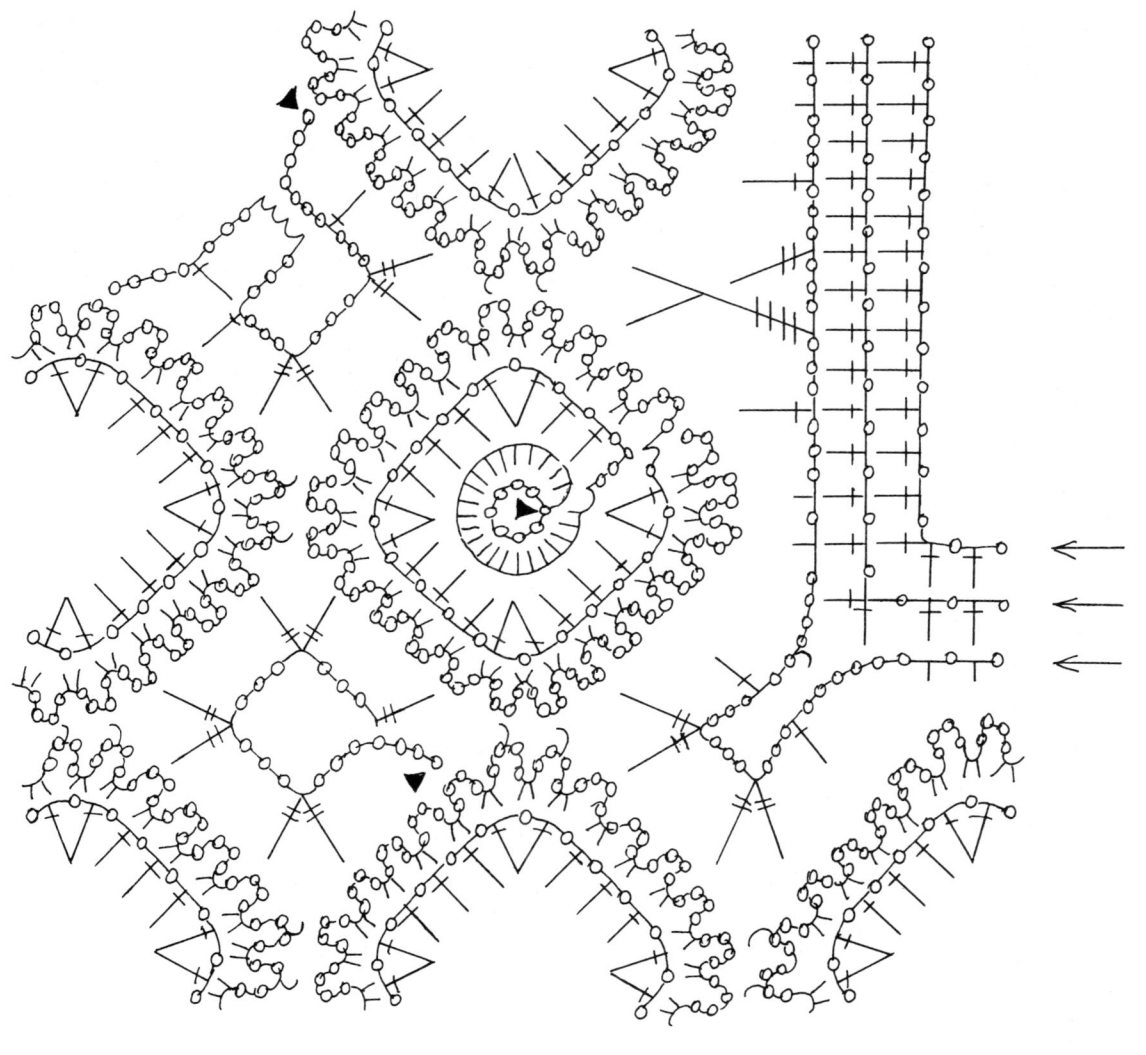

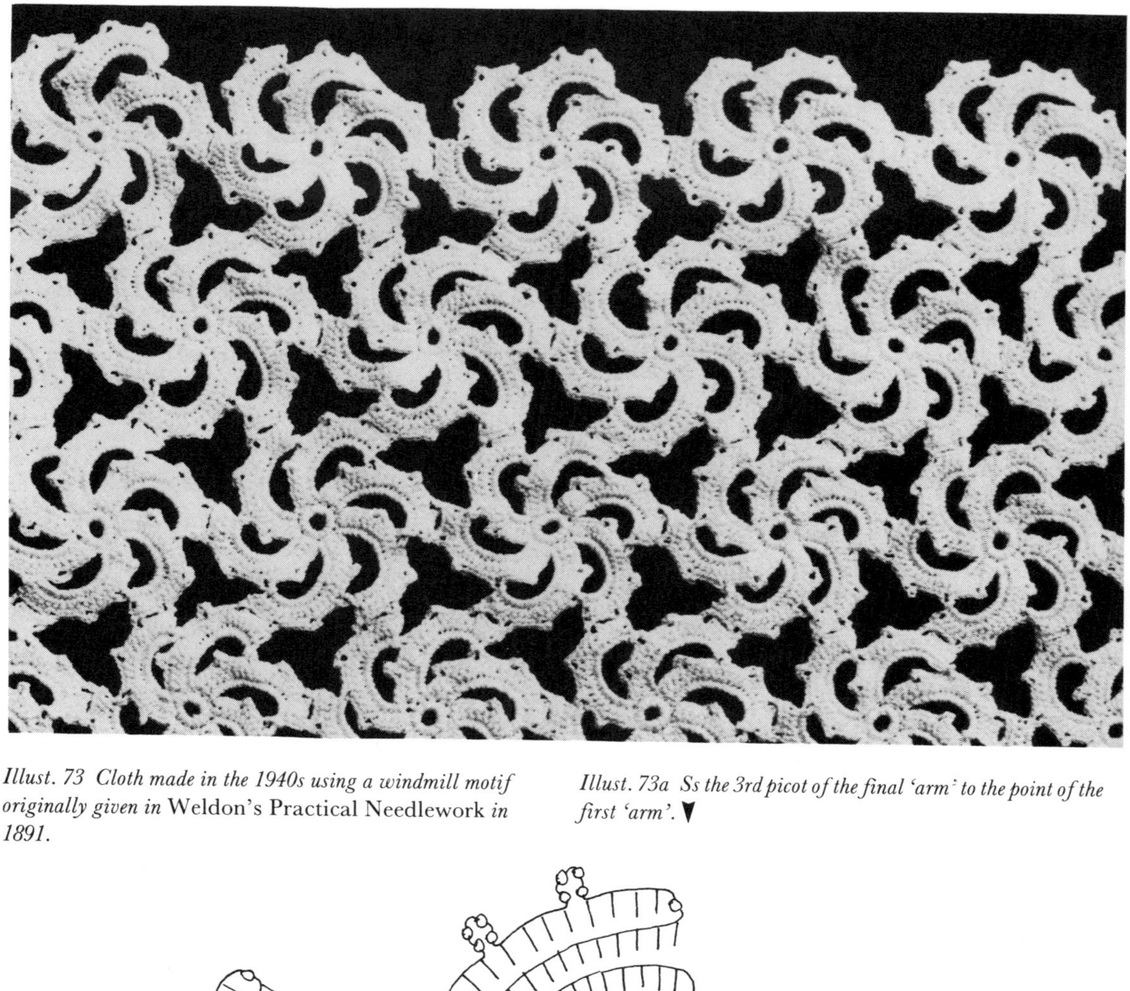

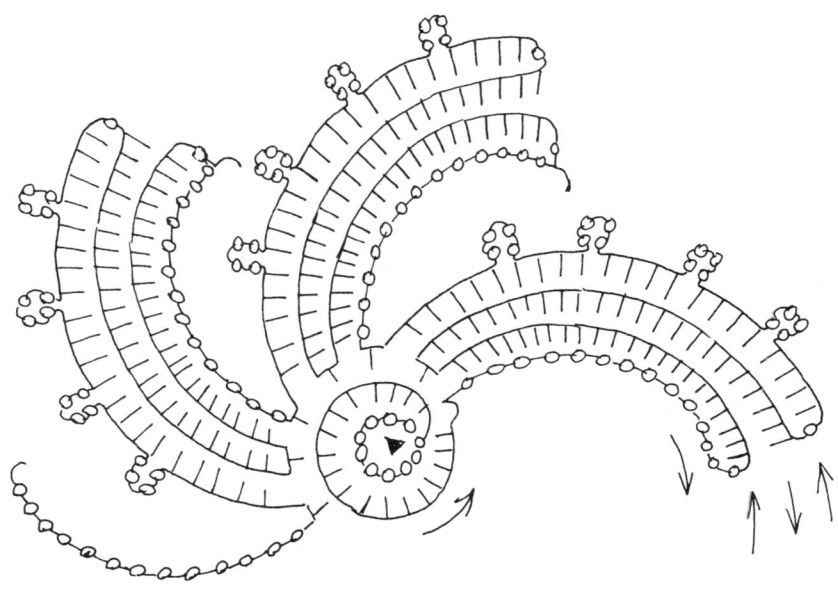

Illust. 73 Cloth made in the 1940s using a windmill motif originally given in Weldon's Practical Needlework *in 1891.*

Illust. 73a Ss the 3rd picot of the final 'arm' to the point of the first 'arm'. ▼

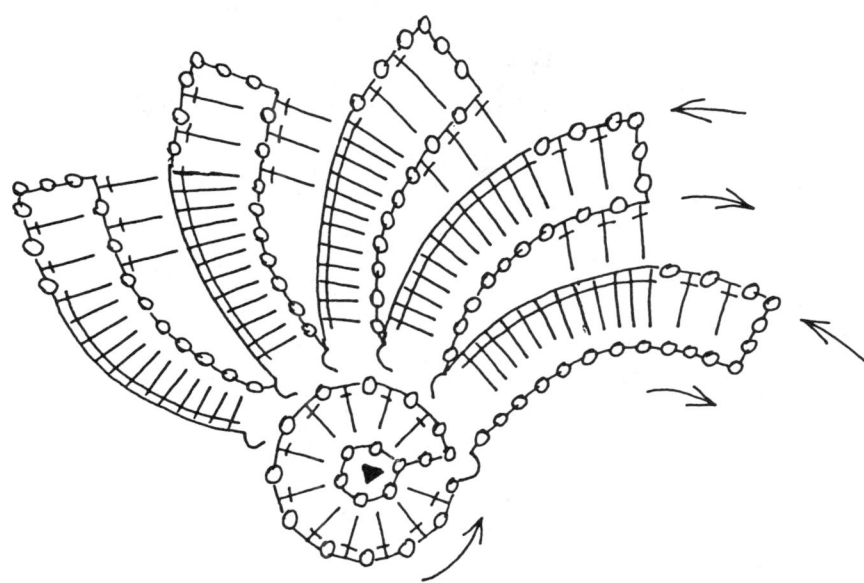

Illust. 74 Cloth made in the 1940s from an older design circa 1918. ▼

Illust. 74a After completing the 12th 'arm' of the windmill, ss back across the last 8 tr, turn the motif upside down and work the 3 missing tr underneath the first 'arm'.

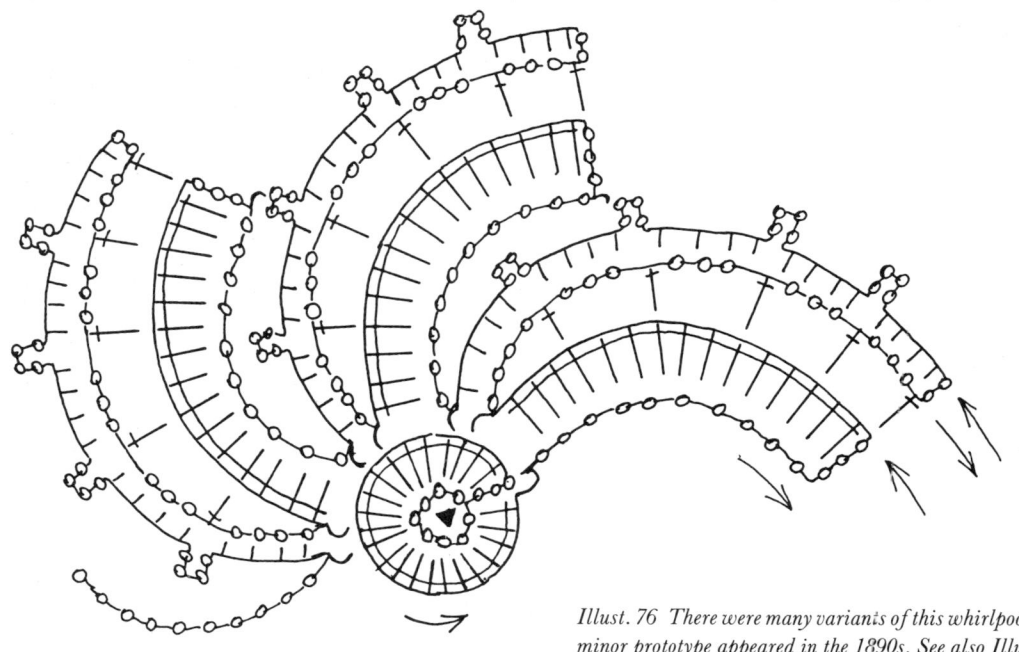

Illust. 75 Cloth made in the 1940s from an earlier design.

Illust. 75a Join the final 'arm' of each motif to its first 'arm' when working the appropriate 4 ch loop. ▼

Illust. 76 There were many variants of this whirlpool motif. A ► *minor prototype appeared in the 1890s. See also Illust. 78.*

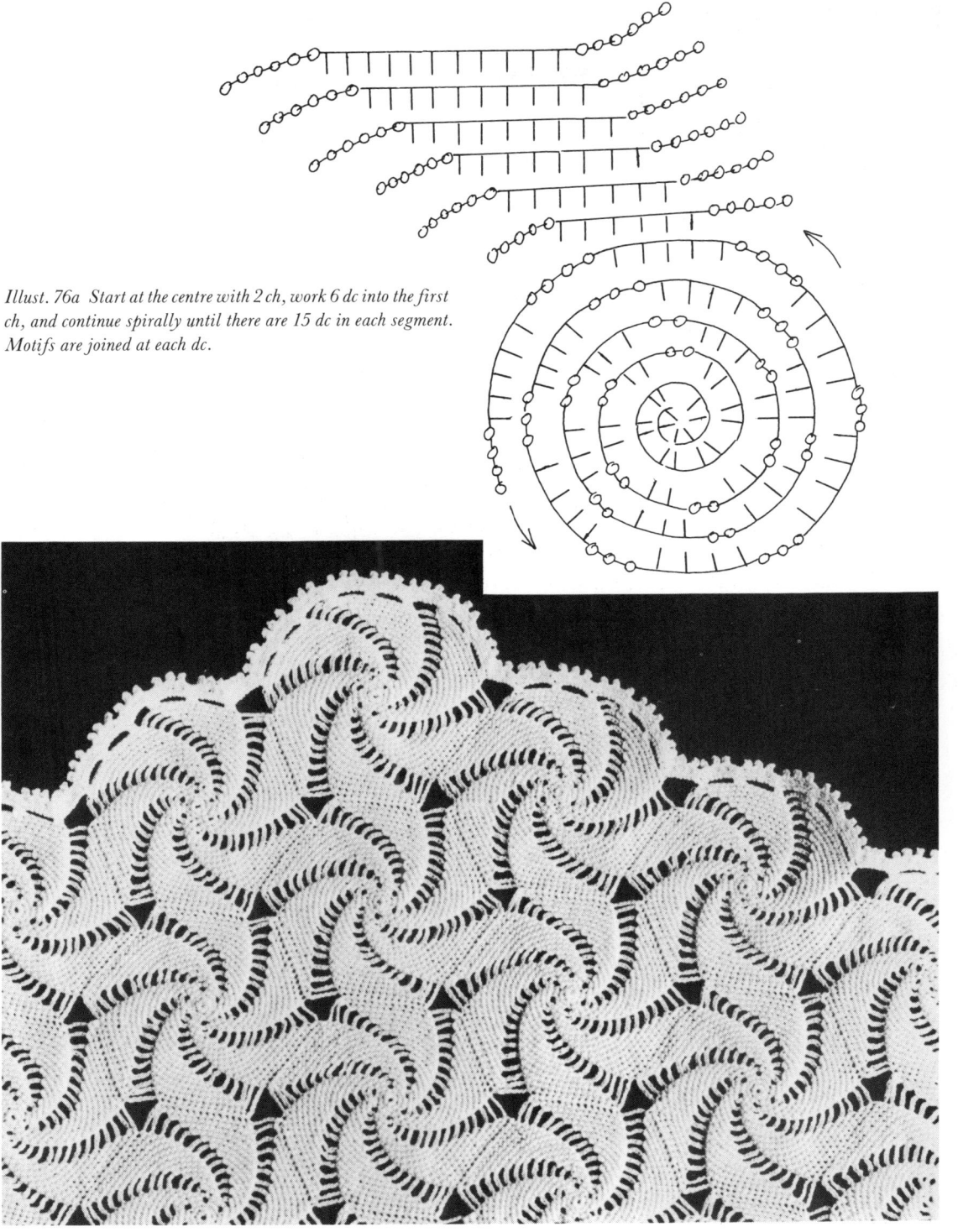

Illust. 76a Start at the centre with 2 ch, work 6 dc into the first ch, and continue spirally until there are 15 dc in each segment. Motifs are joined at each dc.

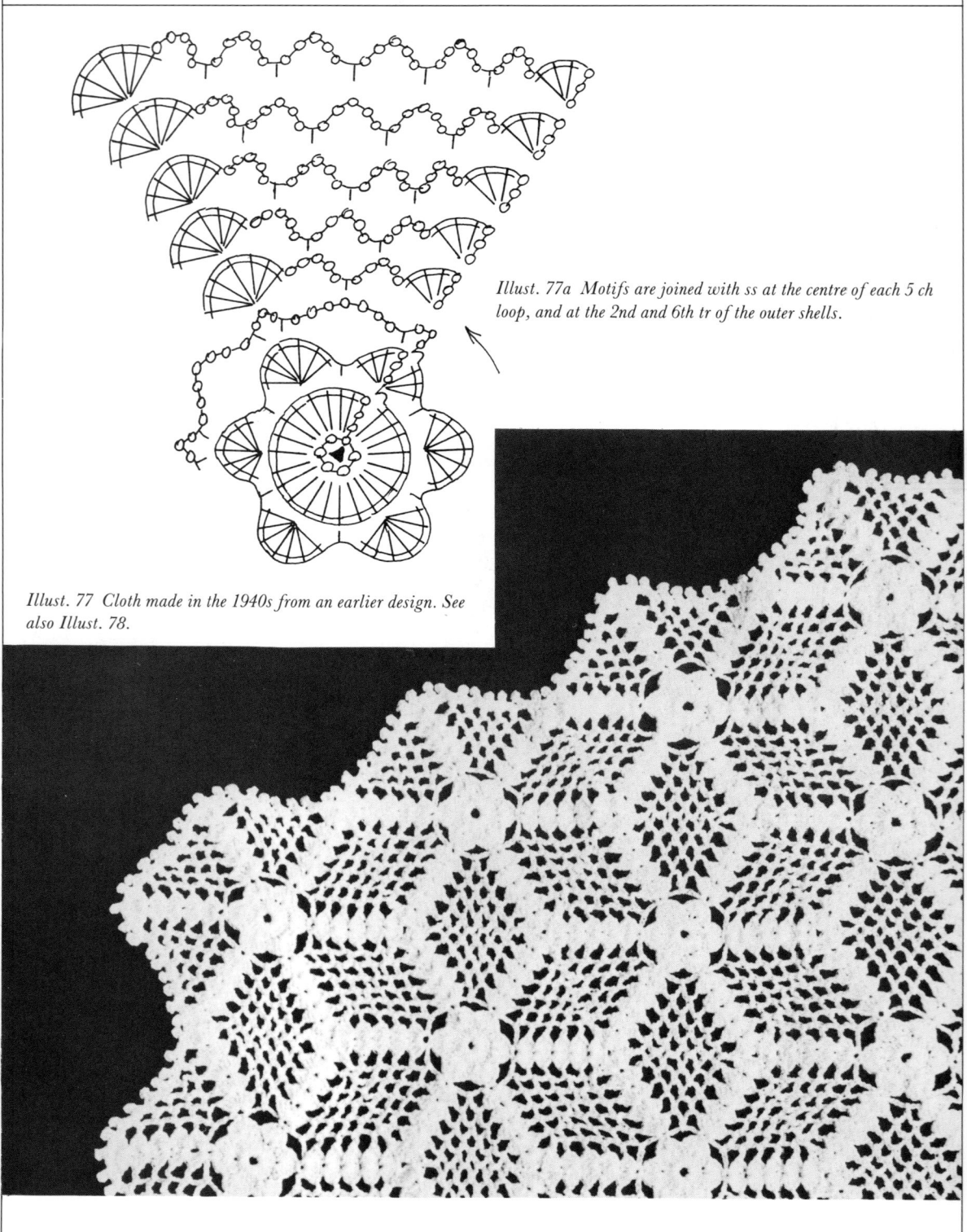

Illust. 77a Motifs are joined with ss at the centre of each 5 ch loop, and at the 2nd and 6th tr of the outer shells.

Illust. 77 Cloth made in the 1940s from an earlier design. See also Illust. 78.

Illust. 78 The smallest motif is a reticella wheel.

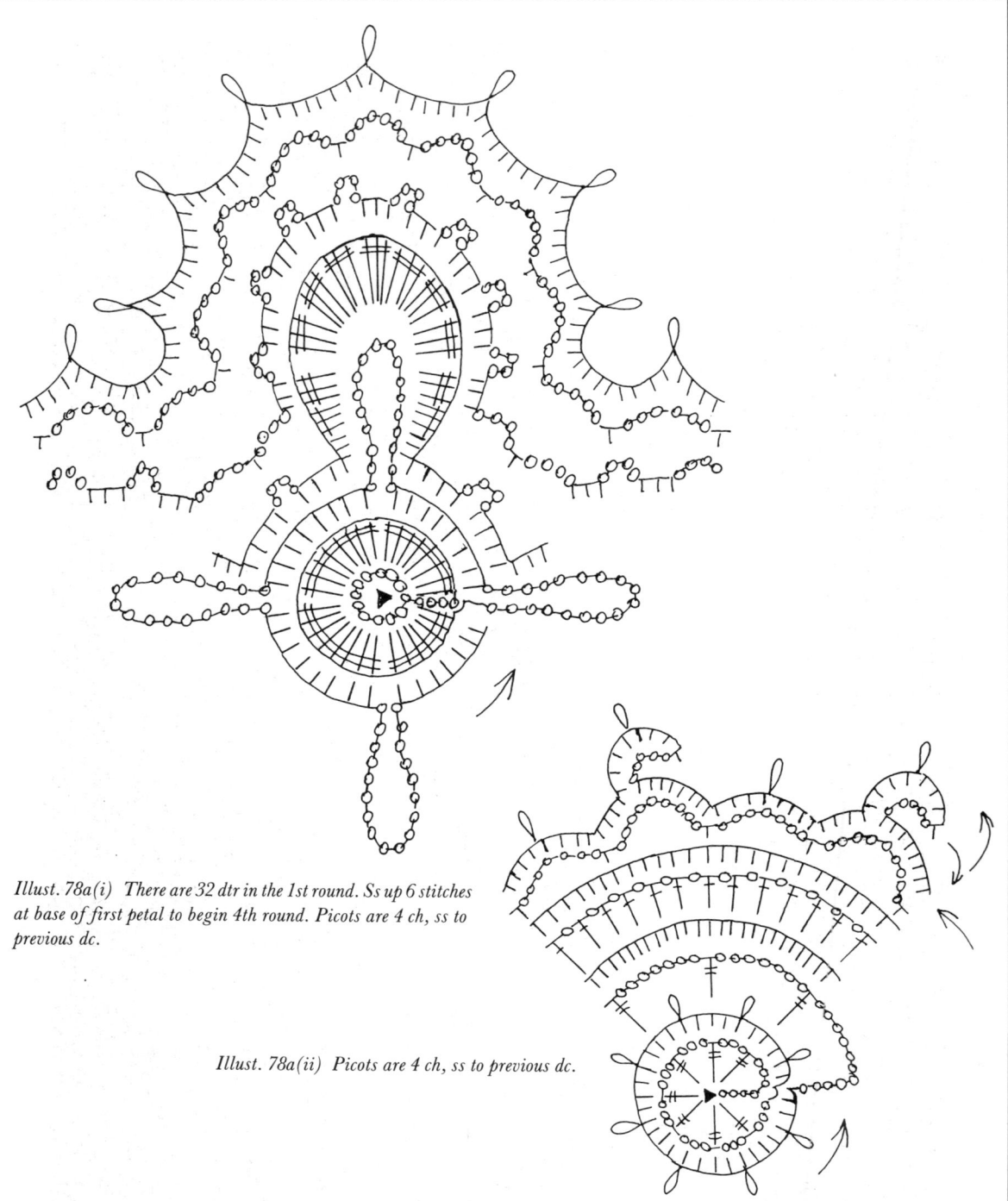

Illust. 78a(i) There are 32 dtr in the 1st round. Ss up 6 stitches at base of first petal to begin 4th round. Picots are 4 ch, ss to previous dc.

Illust. 78a(ii) Picots are 4 ch, ss to previous dc.

Illust. 79 The square motif is a reticella design. The scallop- ➤ *shell motif was found on the neck tie of a blouse.*

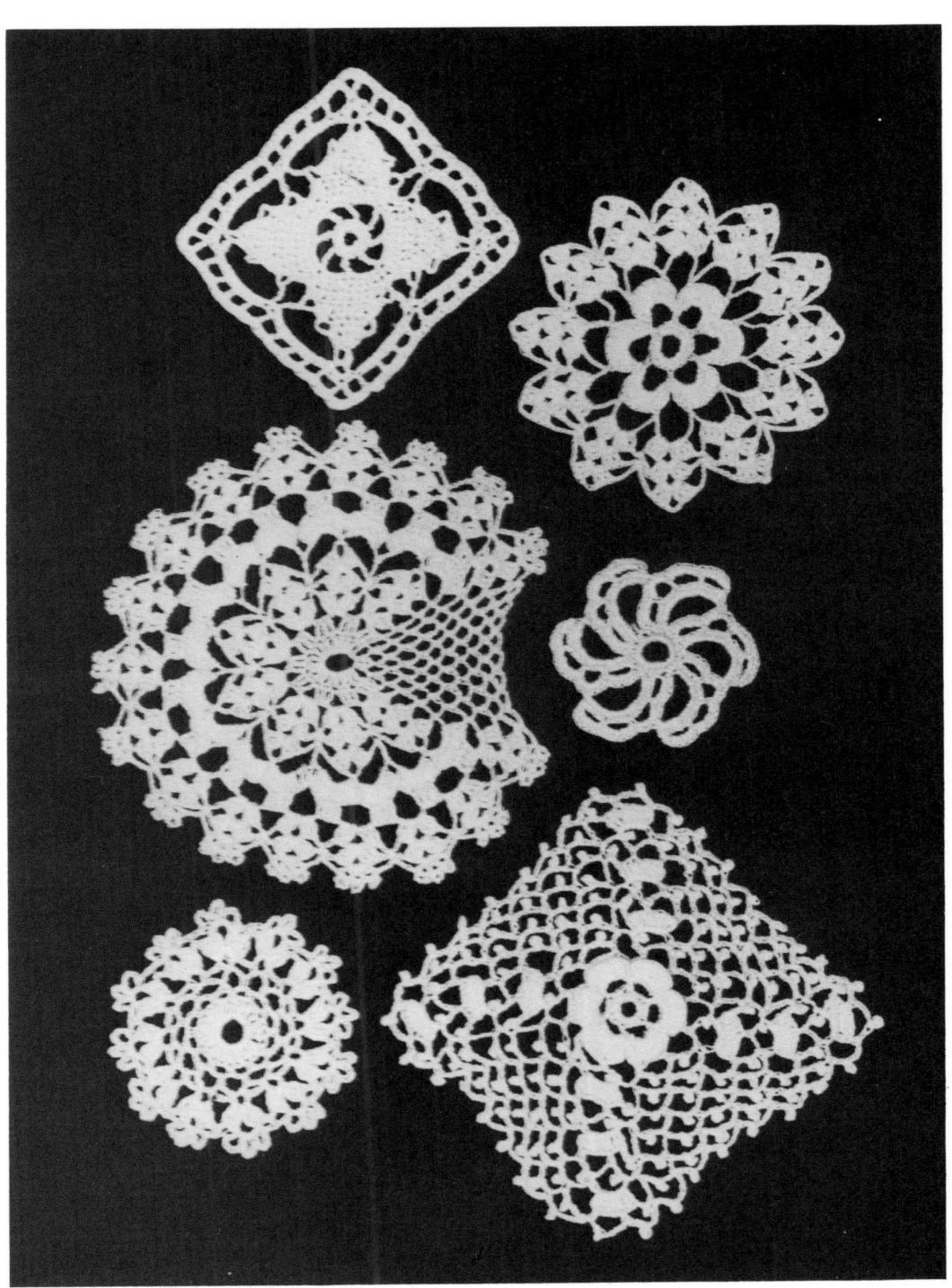

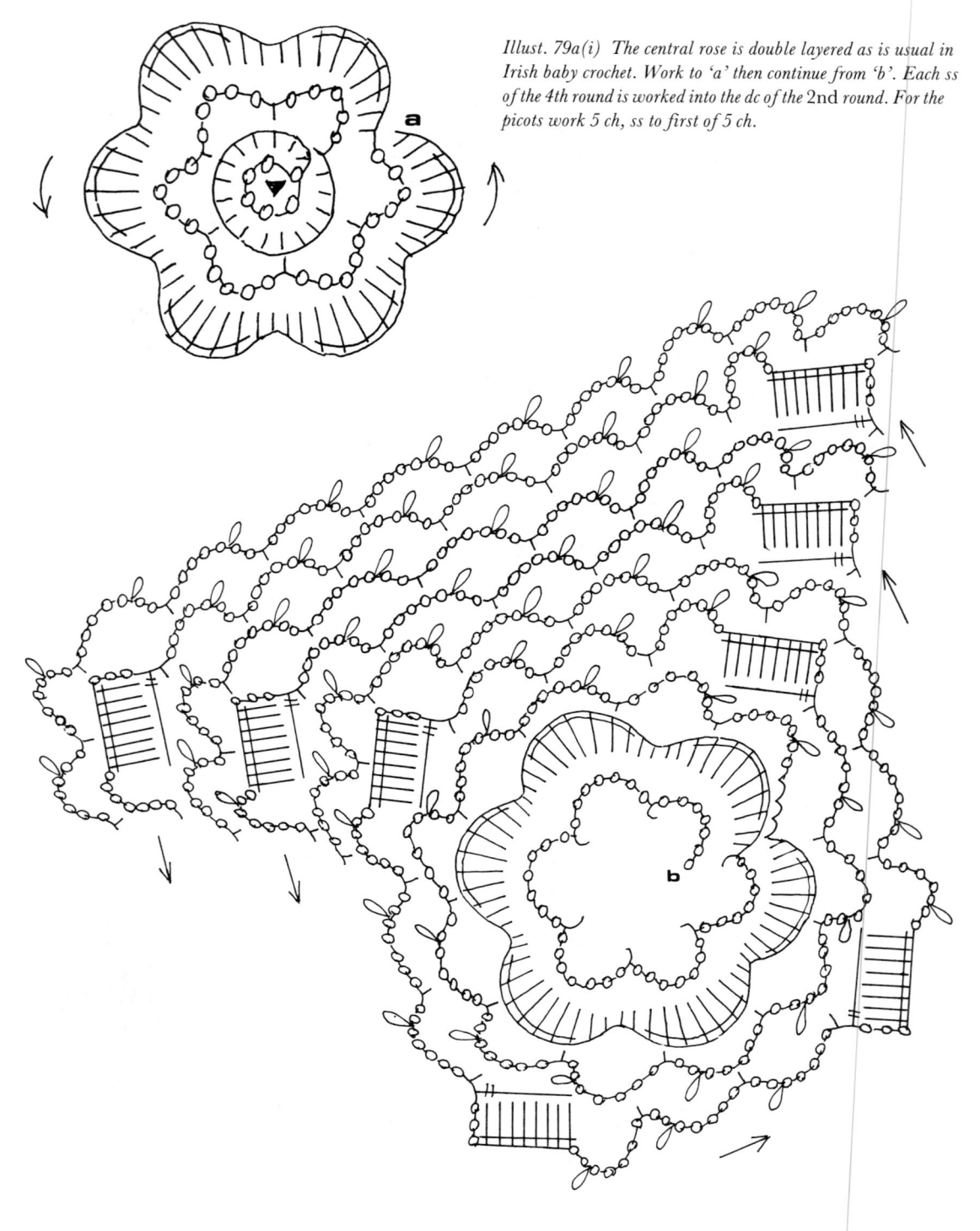

Illust. 79a(i) The central rose is double layered as is usual in Irish baby crochet. Work to 'a' then continue from 'b'. Each ss of the 4th round is worked into the dc of the 2nd round. For the picots work 5 ch, ss to first of 5 ch.

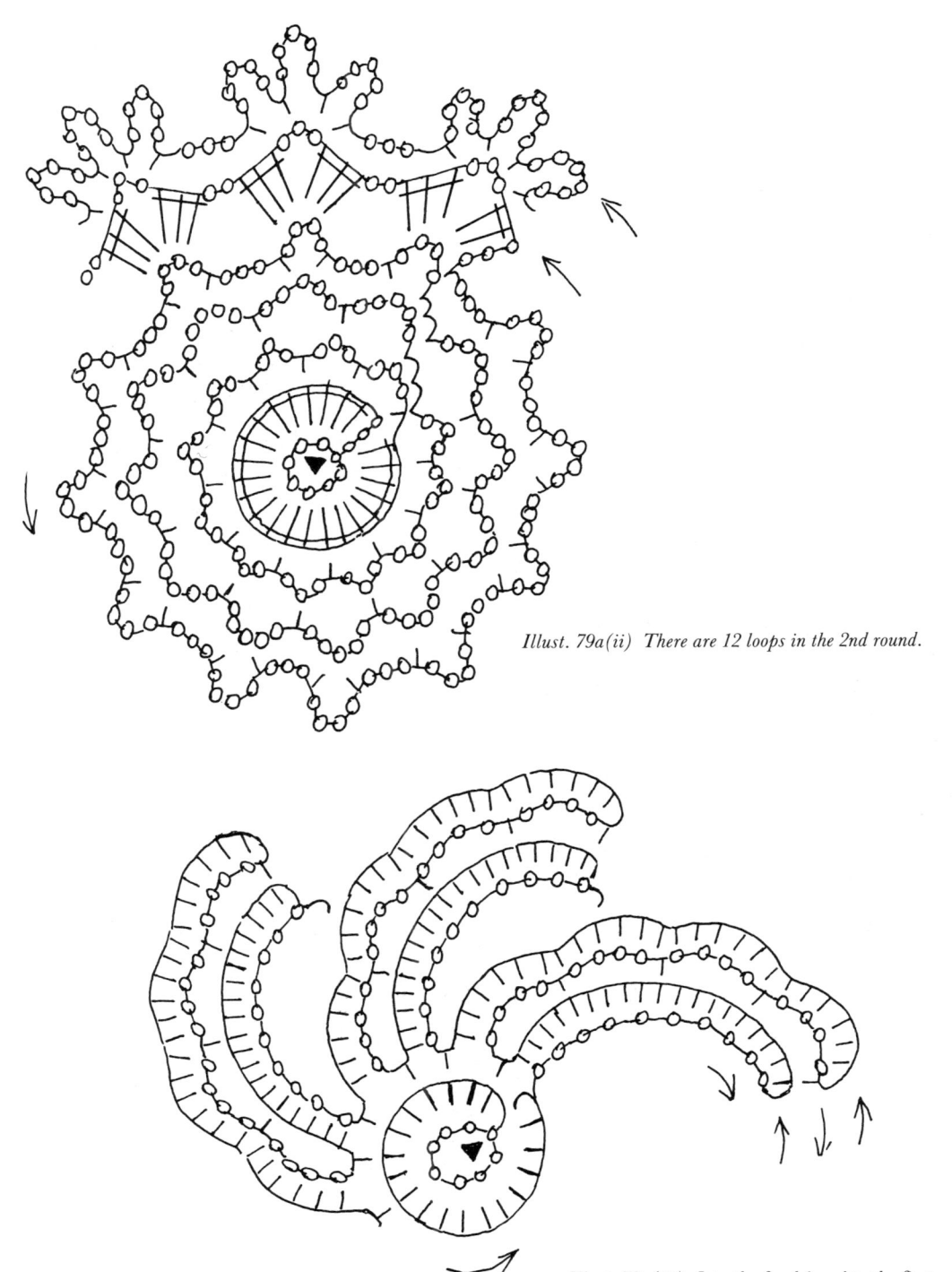

Illust. 79a(ii) There are 12 loops in the 2nd round.

Illust. 79a(iii) Join the final 'arm' to the first with ss.

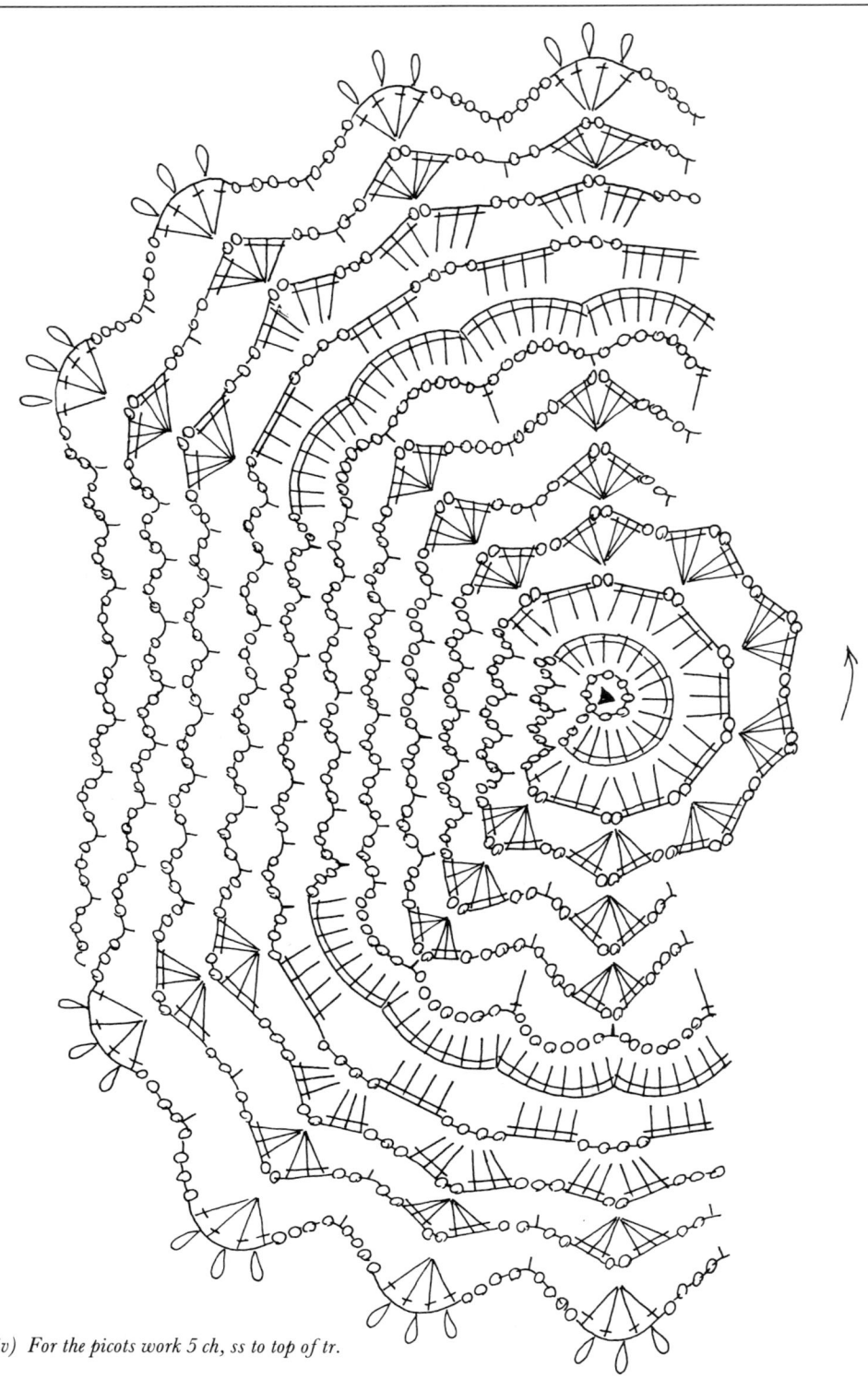

Illust. 79a(iv) For the picots work 5 ch, ss to top of tr.

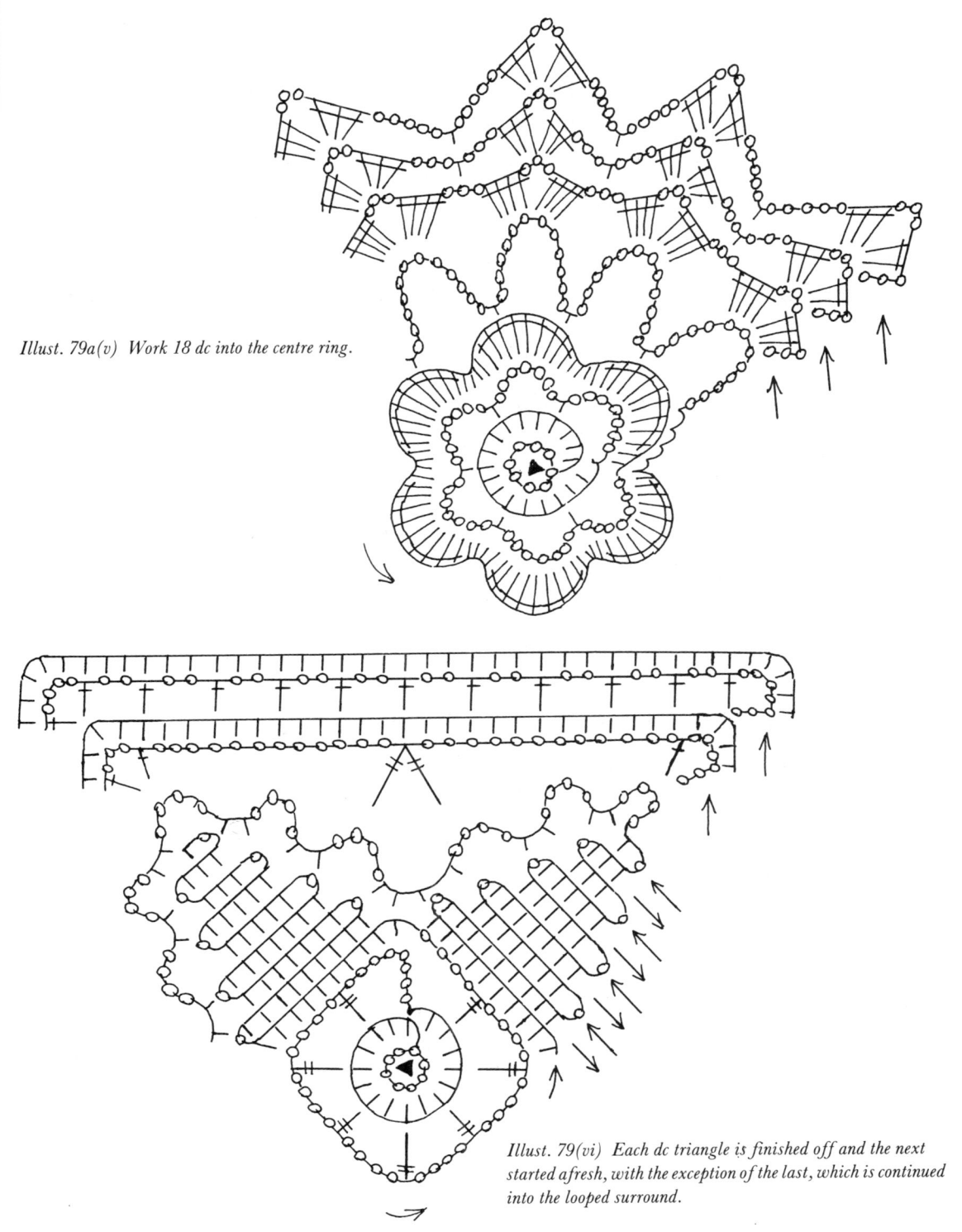

Illust. 79a(v) Work 18 dc into the centre ring.

Illust. 79(vi) Each dc triangle is finished off and the next started afresh, with the exception of the last, which is continued into the looped surround.

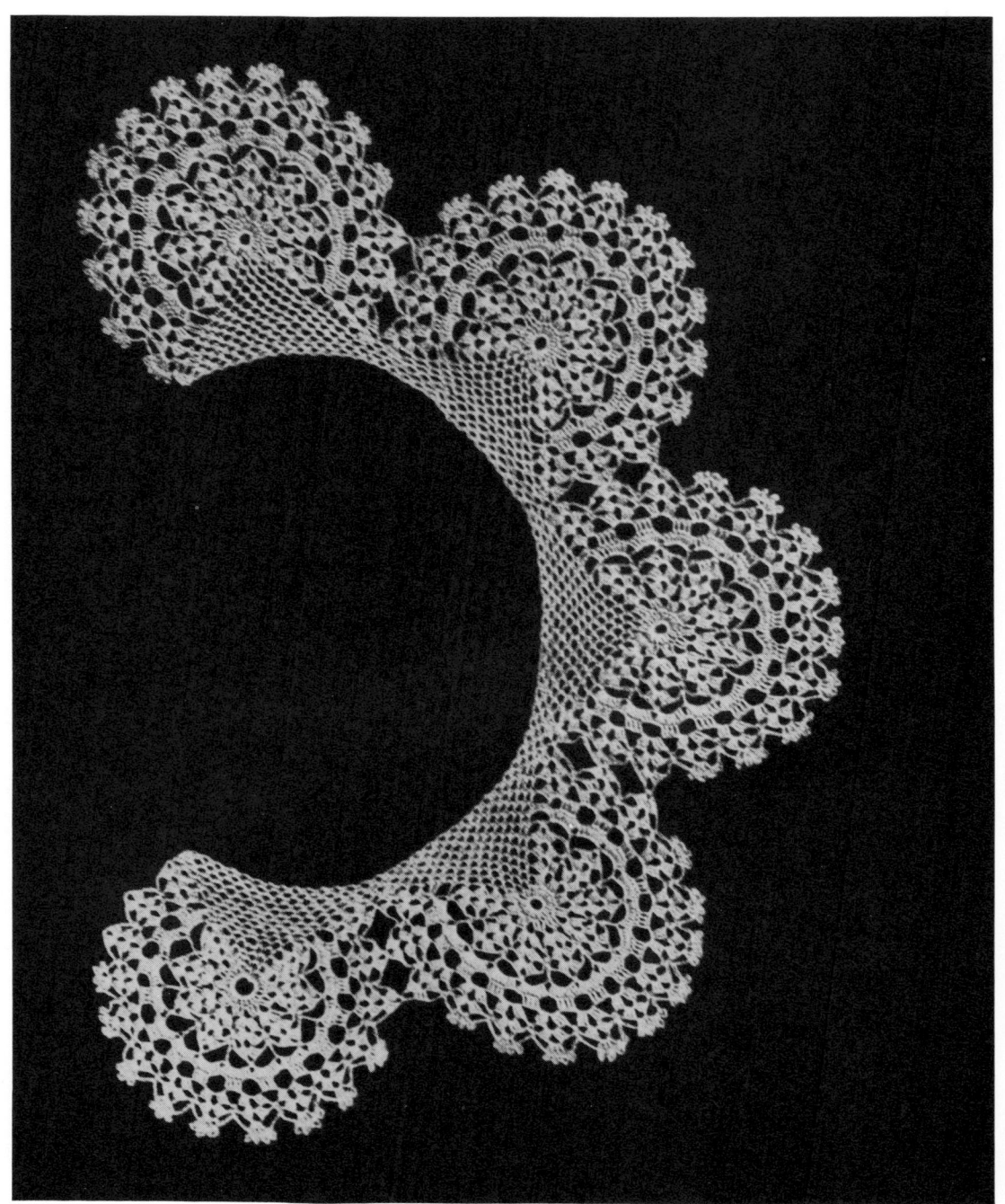

Illust. 80 This late-1920s collar is a variant of Illust. 79a (iv).

*Illust. 80a Motifs are joined with ss at the 3 top points. For the ▶
picots work 5 ch, ss to top of tr. To finish the collar, work 3 rows
of the 3 ch mesh on the inner edge, connecting all motifs.*

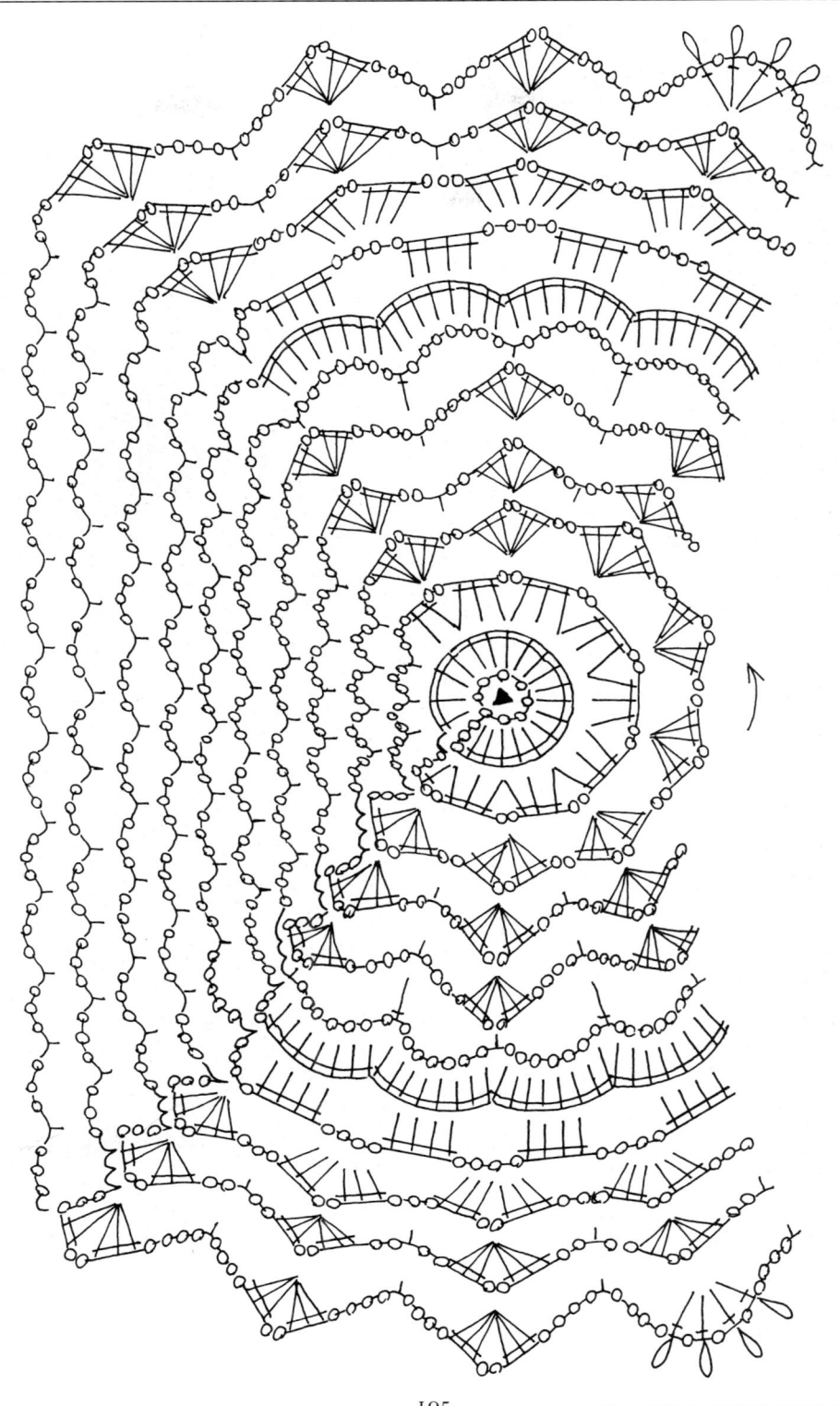

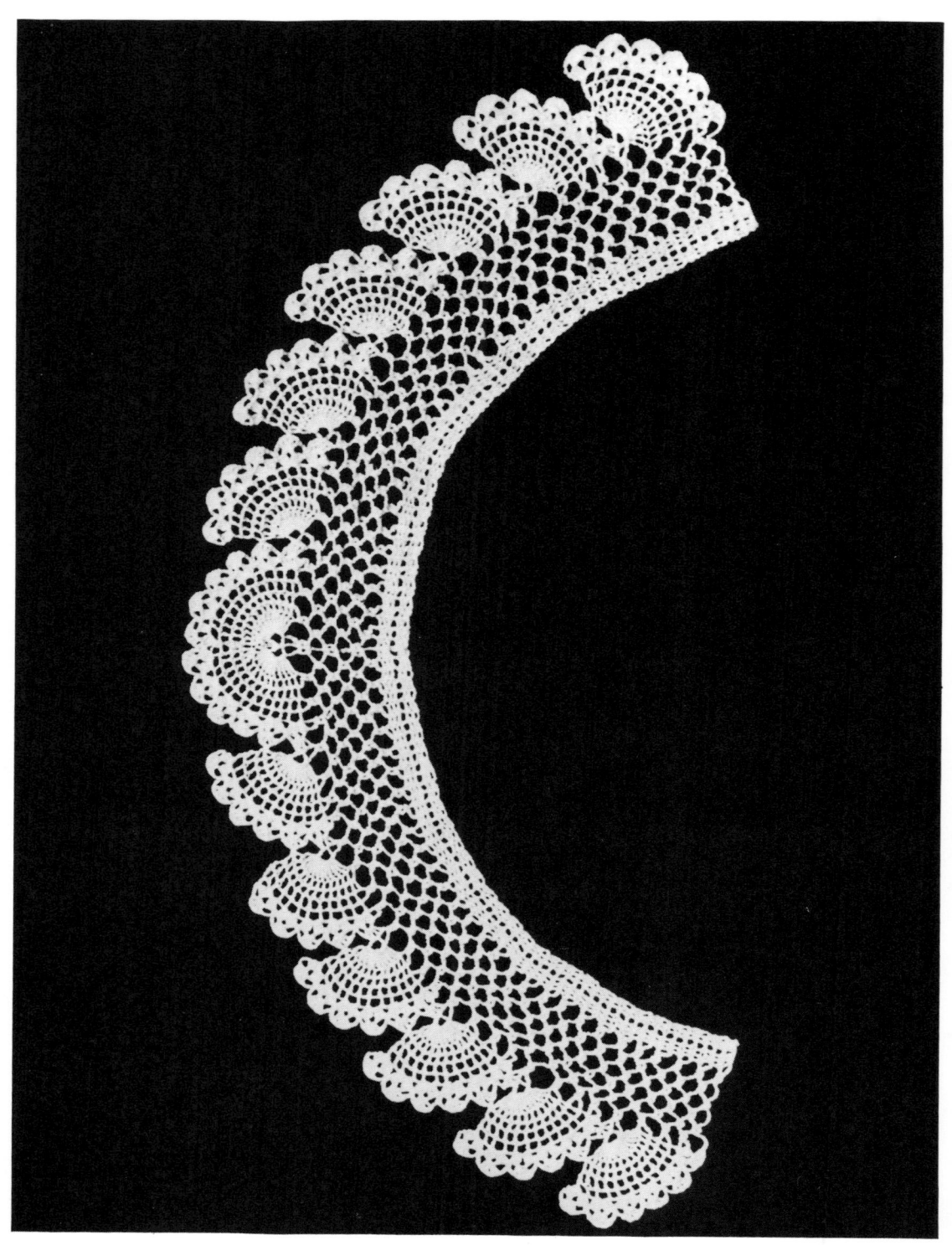

◄ *Illust. 81 Collar, late 1920s.*

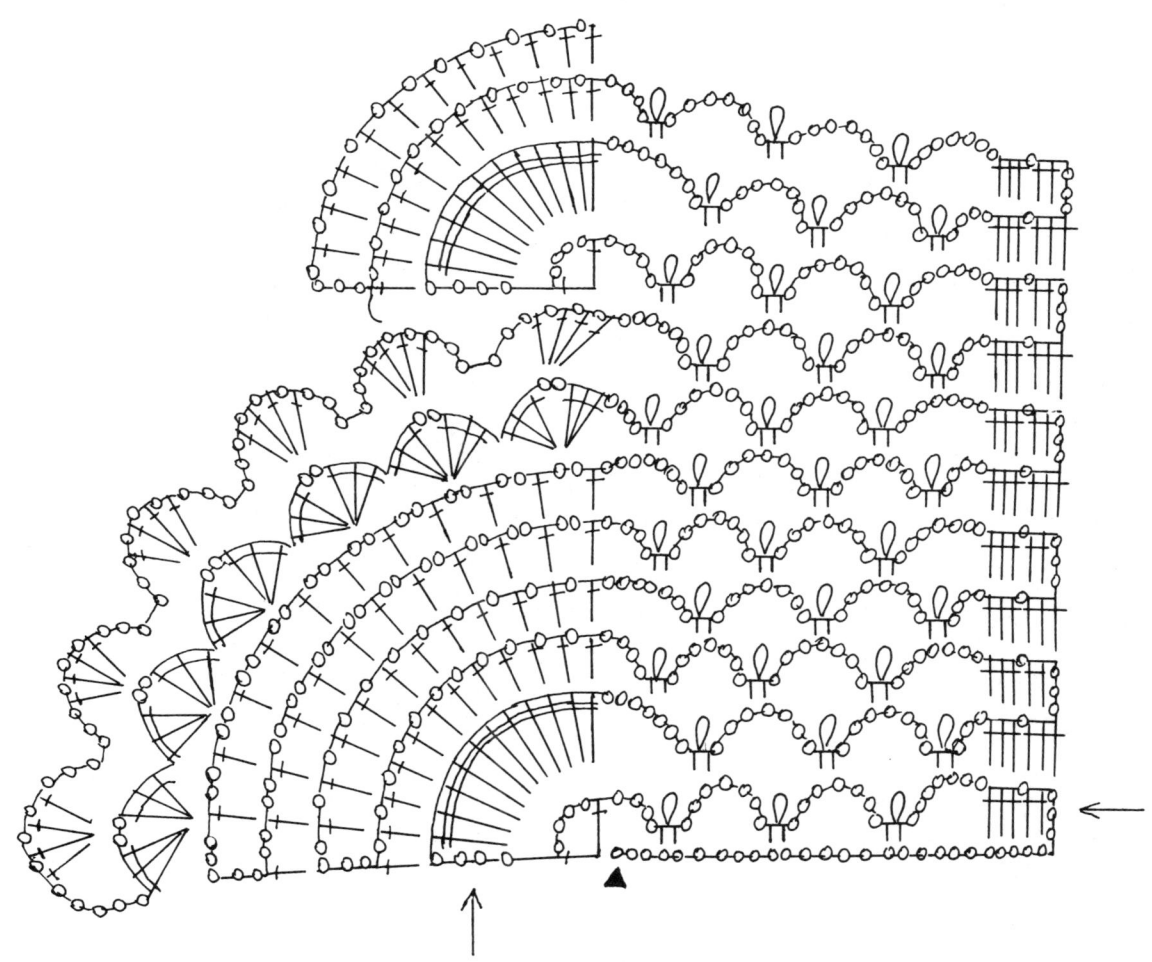

Illust. 81a Start at the centre back. For the picots work 3 ch between the 2 dc.

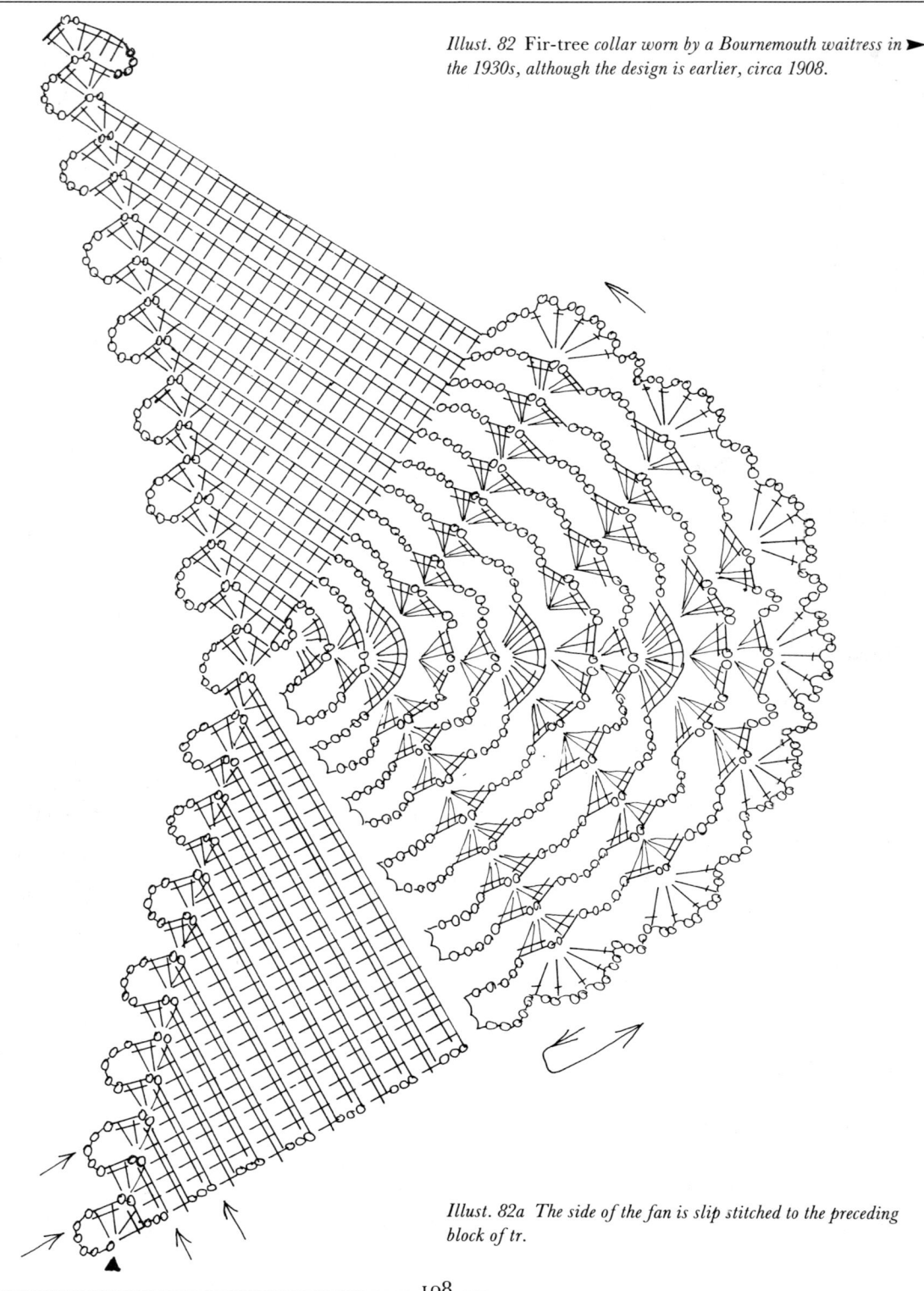

Illust. 82 Fir-tree *collar worn by a Bournemouth waitress in the 1930s, although the design is earlier, circa 1908.*

Illust. 82a The side of the fan is slip stitched to the preceding block of tr.

Lady's Gloves 1

These gloves will adapt to different sizes. On completion shrink them in hot water, then stretch to the size required. Use mercerised crochet cotton No. 60 and a hook size 0.75 mm.

RIGHT-HAND GLOVE

Start with 3 ch, 1 tr into first chain made, * 3 ch, 1 tr between previous tr and ch. Repeat from * to make a foundation of 60 loops. Join last to first with ss.

1st Round: (7 ch, miss 1 loop, 1 dc into next loop) 30 times.

2nd and 3rd Rounds: (7 ch, 1 dc into next loop) 30 times.

4th Round: Increase by working 2 loops into the first loop of round.

5th Round: Work without increase.

Repeat 4th and 5th Rounds until there are seven increases altogether, then work one more round without increase.

Illust. 83 The cuffs are worked in wheat-ear crochet. ➤

Illust. 83a Each 'wheat grain' is a cluster of 4 dtr.

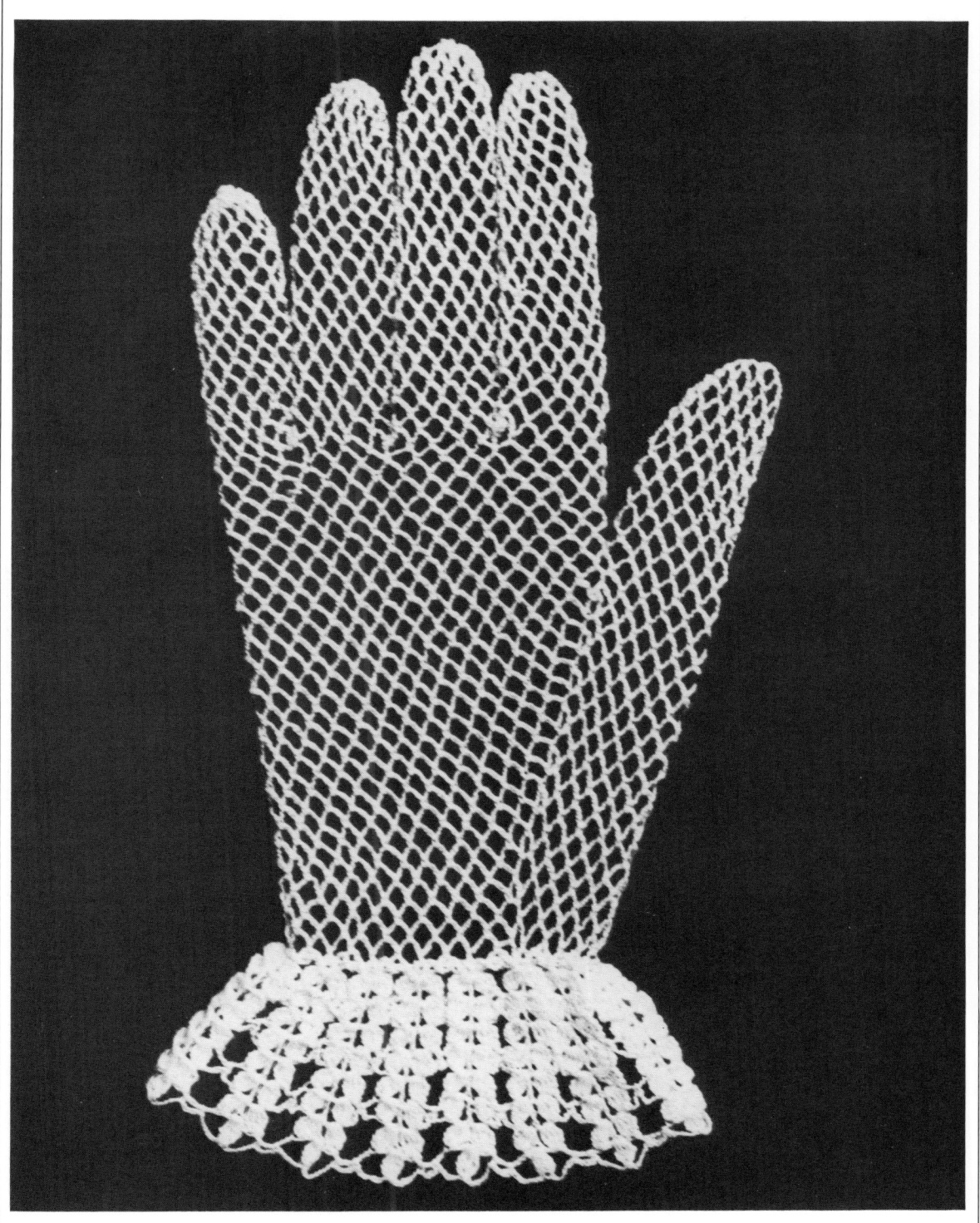

Thumb: Work 15 ch, miss 27 loops, 1 dc into 28th, and continue around, working 2 loops across 15 ch (making 11 loops in each round) for 14 rounds, or length required. Shape top by working 2 rounds of 4 ch instead of 7 ch. Finish off, drawing the tip together with a needle.

Join to front of palm at base of thumb, and continue in rounds of 30 loops (including 2 across the base of thumb) for 11 rounds.

1st Finger: Work 4 loops at beginning of round, 15 ch, miss 21 loops, 1 dc into 22nd, and continue around, working 2 loops across 15 ch (making 10 loops in each round) for 20 rounds, or length required. Shape top as for thumb.

2nd Finger: With palm facing, join to dc at base of 1st Finger. Work 4 loops, 7 ch, miss 13 loops, 1 dc into 14th, and continue around, working only one loop across base of 1st Finger (making 10 loops in each round), for 22 rounds, or length required. Shape top as before.

3rd Finger: With palm facing, join to dc at base of 2nd Finger. Work 3 loops, 15 ch, miss 6 loops, 1 dc into 7th, and continue around, working one loop across base of 2nd Finger and 2 loops across 15 ch (making 10 loops in each round), for 20 rounds, or length required. Shape top as before.

4th Finger: With palm facing, join to dc at base of 3rd Finger. Work 17 rounds of 9 loops, or length required. Shape top as before.

LEFT-HAND GLOVE
Work exactly as right-hand glove and turn inside-out when finished.

CUFFS
Follow diagram, working a double-leaf group into every 4th loop of foundation. Thread a strand of shirring elastic through the foundation loops.

Lady's Gloves 2
Work hands as Lady's Gloves 1. For the cuffs, work 5 rounds as 1st to 5th Rounds of hand, then continue from the diagram. Thread a strand of shirring elastic through the foundation loops.

Illust. 84 The same glove with an alternative cuff, late 1930s. ▶

Illust. 84a For the picots work 5 ch, ss to top of tr.

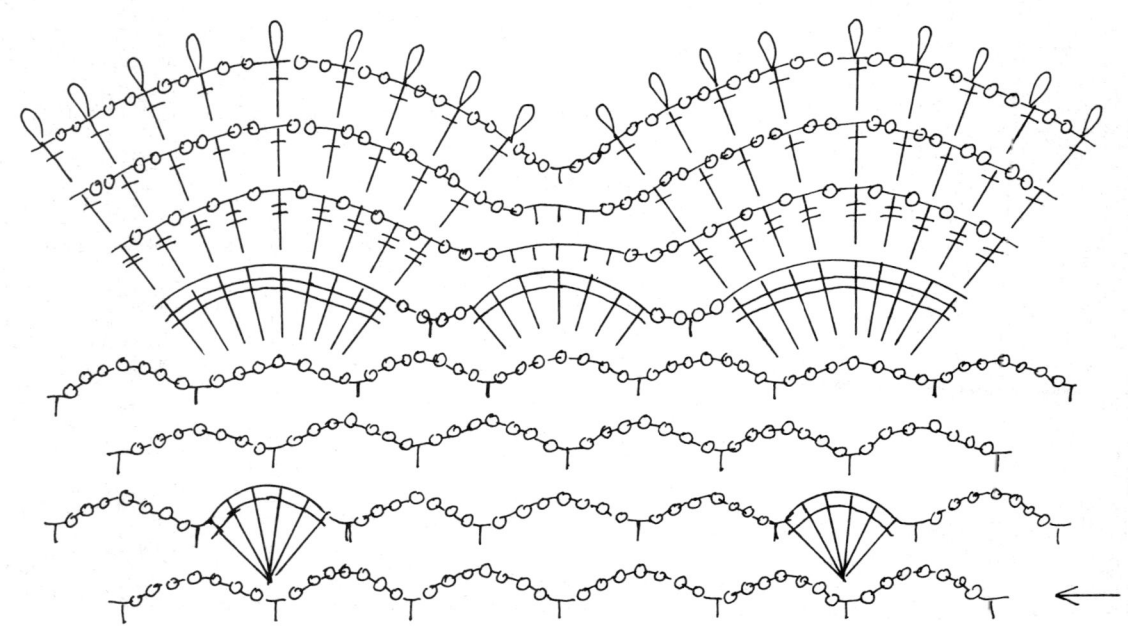

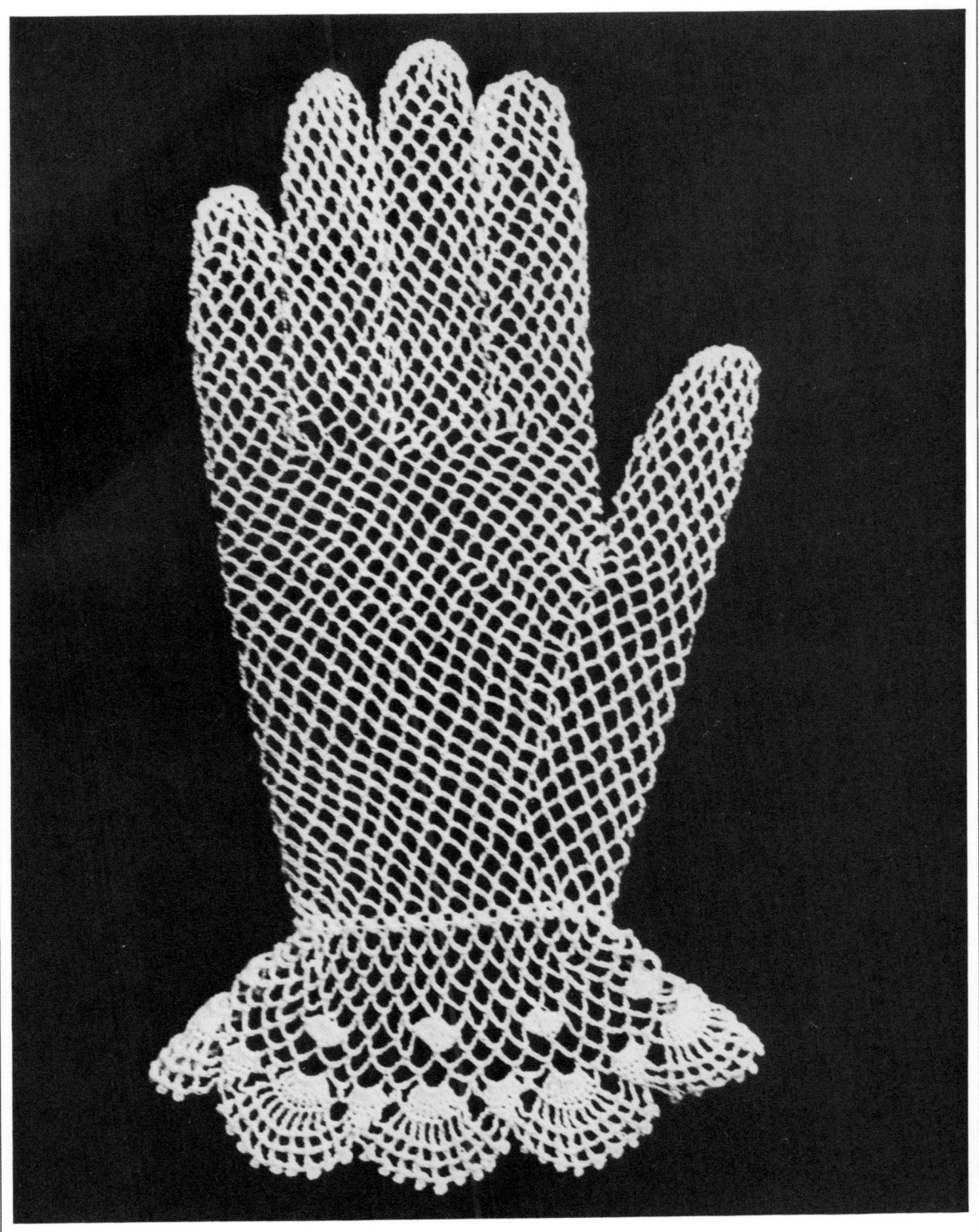

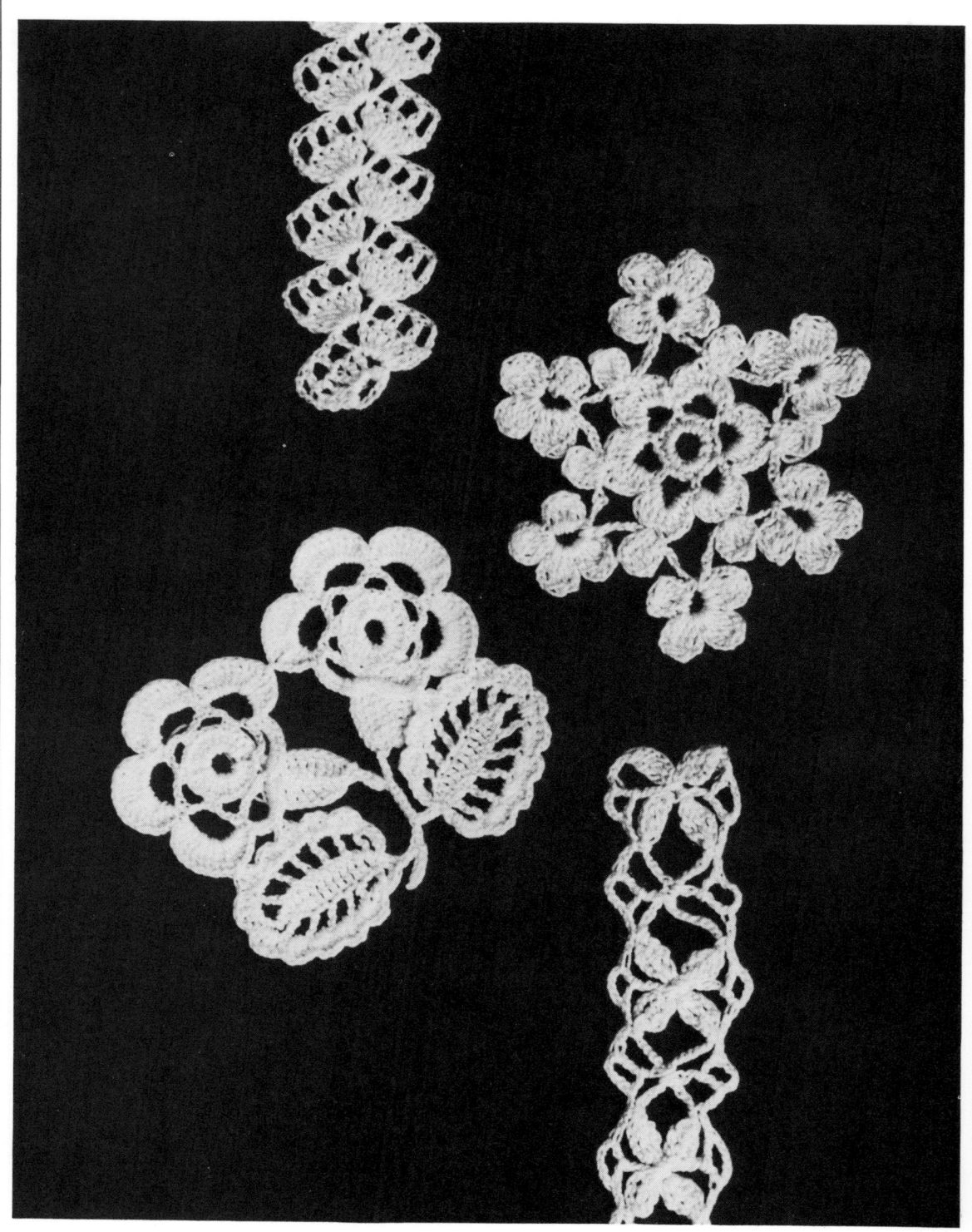

◄ *Illust. 85 The primrose spray is Honiton crochet. The lower braid, called a beading, is intended for threading with ribbon, and is a minor example of Maltese crochet, circa 1912.*

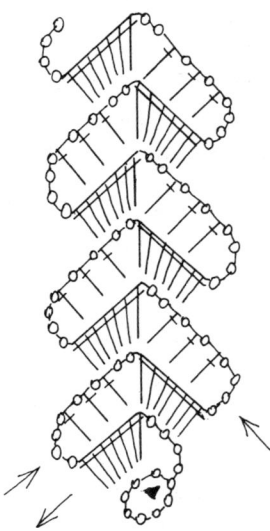

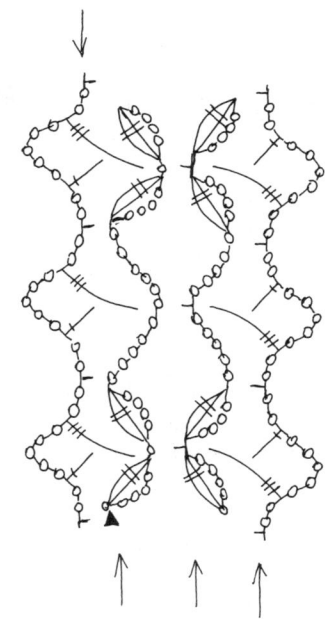

Illust. 85a(i) There are 7 tr in each block.

Illust. 85a(ii) Work the 2 centre rows first.

Illust. 85a(iii) The clusters are 3 dtr.

Illust. 85a(iv) The calyx is sewn underneath the flower afterwards.

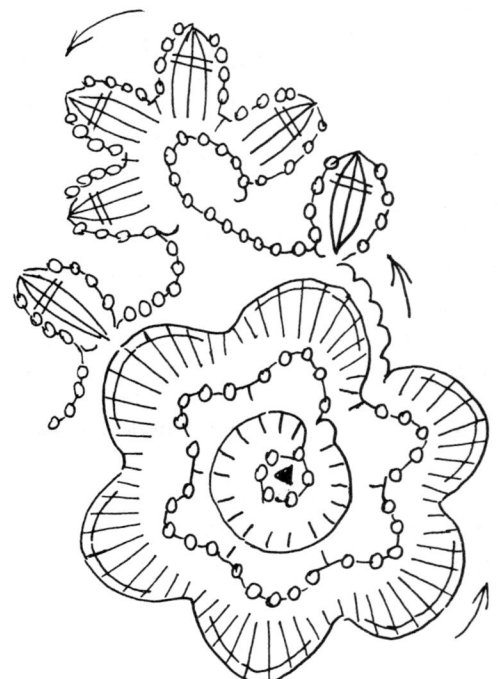

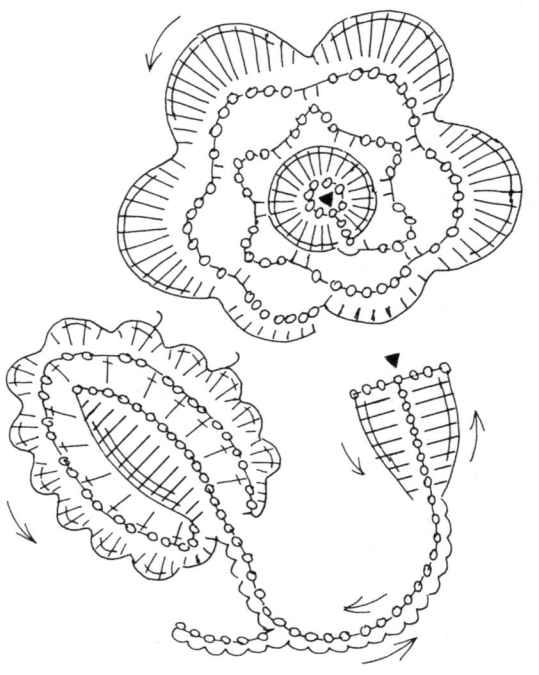

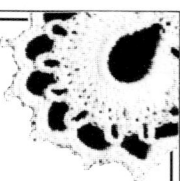

REFERENCES

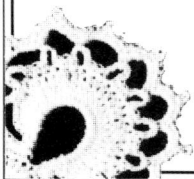

INTRODUCTION

1 *Aunt Kate's Crochet Work*, published by John Leng and Co., Dundee and London. 'Aunt Kate' was the pseudonym of Helen Greig Souter.

CHAPTER 1 – HISTORICAL DEVELOPMENT OF TECHNIQUE

1 Published by Art Needlework Industries Ltd., 1967.
2 'Classification of Basic Textile Techniques', *Ciba Review*, 1948, No. 63.
3 Santina M. Levey, *Lace – A History*, Victoria and Albert Museum, 1983.
4 Victoria and Albert Museum accession number T24 1980.
5 Mrs Bury Pallister, *History of Lace*, 1875, revised edition 1902.
6 Ibid.
7 Pat Earnshaw, *A Dictionary of Lace*, Shire Publications Ltd, 1982.
8 Mlle Riego, in *Crochet Book*, 2nd Series, 1848, describes slip stitch worked in rows as 'single crochet or shepherd's knitting'.
9 *Janet's Repentance*, a story from *Scenes of Clerical Life*, which first appeared in *Blackwood's Magazine*.

CHAPTER 2 – HISTORICAL DEVELOPMENT OF DESIGN

1 First printed in 1931, reprinted by Batsford in 1983. Margaret Maidment's lace designs were traditional, and were of older origin than the date of her first publication suggests.

CHAPTER 3 – IRISH CROCHET

1 *Catalogue to the Collection of Lace*, National Museum of Ireland.
Irish Lace, Irish Heritage Series No. 21, Eason and Son Ltd, Dublin, 1978.
2 *The Irish Flowerers*, Ulster Folk Museum and the Institute of Irish Studies, 1971.
3 Mrs Meredith, *The Lacemakers*, 1865.
4 *The Selected Works of Mdlle Riego*, Vol 2, edited and revised by Mrs Rivers-Turnbull 1905.
5 Maria Mies, *The Lacemakers of Narsapur*, Zed Press, 1982.

CHAPTER 4 – MORE TYPES OF CROCHET

1 *Anchor Manual of Needlework*, B.T. Batsford Ltd, 3rd edition, 1968.
2 J. & P. Coats Ltd, published a collection of patterns under this name in 1967.
3 Flora Klickmann, *The Craft of the Crochet Hook*, 1912.
4 Sylvia Groves, *The History of Needlework Tools and Accessories*, Hamlyn, 1966.
5 Thérèse de Dillmont, *Encyclopedia of Needlework*, 1886.
6 Ann Stearns, *The Batsford Book of Crochet*, B.T. Batsford Ltd, 1981.

CHAPTER 5 – MATERIALS AND EQUIPMENT

1 Published in *Bestway* Series 208, in the early 1930s.
2 British Patent Specification No. 12370, (1848).
3 British Patent Specification No. 22169, (1912).

CHAPTER 6 – PRESERVATION AND STORAGE

1 The Fabric Care Research Association Ltd recommend soap flakes or *Stergene*.
2 Published by Barrie and Jenkins, 1977.

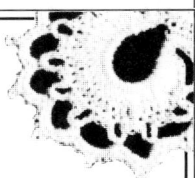

BIBLIOGRAPHY

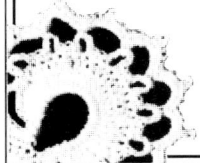

GENERAL

Boyle, Elizabeth, *The Irish Flowerers*, Ulster Folk Museum and the Institute of Irish Studies, 1971.

Groves, Sylvia, *The History of Needlework Tools and Accessories*, Hamlyn, 1966.

Levey, Santina M., *Lace – A History*, Victoria and Albert Museum, 1983.

Longfield, Ada, *Catalogue to the Collection of Lace*, National Museum of Ireland.

Longfield, Ada, *Irish Lace*, Irish Heritage Series 21, Eason and Son Ltd, 1978.

Mies, Maria, *The Lace Makers of Narsapur*, Zed Press, 1982.

Potter, Esther, *English Knitting and Crochet Books of the Nineteenth Century*, Bibliographical Society, 1953.

Rogers, Gay Ann, *An Illustrated History of Needlework Tools*, John Murray, 1983.

Turner, Pauline, *Crochet*, Shire Album 126, 1984.

Wardle, Patricia, *Victorian Lace*, Herbert Jenkins, 1968.

Whiting, Gertrude, *Old-Time Tools and Toys of Needlework*, Columbia University Press, 1928, Dover Publications Inc., 1971.

TECHNIQUES

Anchor Manual of Needlework, B.T. Batsford Ltd, 3rd edition, 1968.

d'Arcy, Eithne, *Irish Crochet Lace*, Dolmen Press, 1984, Dryad Press, 1985.

Maidens, Ena, *Techniques of Crocheted and Openwork Lace*, B.T. Batsford Ltd, 1982.

Stearns, Ann, *The Batsford Book of Crochet*, B.T. Batsford Ltd, 1981.

Thompson, Pamela, *Hairpin Crochet; Technique and Design*, B.T. Batsford Ltd, 1984.

PATTERN REPRINTS

Crocheted Art Edgings and Insertions, Some Place Publications (California), 1975.

Crochet Designs of Anne Orr, Dover Publications Inc., 1978.

Irish Crochet (The Priscilla Irish Crochet Book), Dover Publications Inc., 1984.

Victorian Crochet by Weldon and Company, Dover Publications Inc., 1974.

More older publications are cited in Chapter 7.

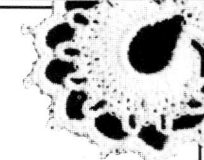

FURTHER INFORMATION

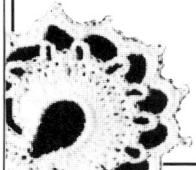

SOME MUSEUM COLLECTIONS OF CROCHET LACE

Preliminary enquiry is recommended as some collections may be in store rather than on display.

Armagh County Museum, Armagh
Bowes Museum, Barnard Castle, Co. Durham
Castle Museum, Norwich
Castle Museum, York
Manor Costume Museum, Bexhill, Sussex
Monaghan County Museum, Monaghan
Museum of Childhood, Bethnal Green, London
Museum of Costume and Textiles, Nottingham
National Museum of Ireland, Dublin
Old House Museum, Bakewell, Derbyshire
Rougemont House Museum of Costume and Lace, Exeter
Royal Scottish Museum, Edinburgh
Ulster Folk and Transport Museum, Holywood, Co. Down
Victoria and Albert Museum, South Kensington, London

Welsh Folk Museum, Cardiff

Gawthorpe Hall, Padiham, Lancashire, and the *Royal School of Needlework*, South Kensington, London, have private collections which may be viewed by special arrangement only.

NINETEENTH-CENTURY PORTRAITS OF CROCHET WORKERS

The Crochet Worker, (Miss Mary Ann Purdon), by William Etty, 1849, City of York Art Gallery.

Woman Crocheting, by Pierre-Auguste Renoir, 1877, The Barnes Foundation, Merion, Pennsylvania.

By the Seashore, by Pierre-Auguste Renoir, 1883, The Metropolitan Museum of Art, New York.

A Girl Crocheting, by Pierre-August Renoir, The Philadelphia Museum of Art.

A Girl Crocheting, by Pierre-Auguste Renoir, The Sterling and Francine Clark Art Institute, Williamstown, Massachusetts.

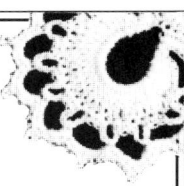

INDEX

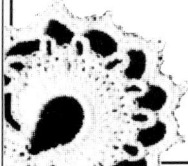

INDEX